111 Places
on the French Riviera
That You Must
Not Miss

emons:

© Emons Verlag GmbH
All rights reserved
© Photographs: Ralf Nestmeyer,
except S. 141, © Var Tourisme, Nicolas Barraquè
© Cover icon: 123rf.com/Irina Tischenko
Design: Eva Kraskes, based on a design
by Lübbeke | Naumann | Thoben
Maps: altancicek.design, www.altancicek.de
English translation: Alan Gentile
Edited by Katrina Fried
Printing and binding: Grafisches Centrum Cuno, Calbe
Printed in Germany 2015
ISBN 978-3-95451-612-4
First edition

Did you enjoy it? Do you want more?
Join us in uncovering new places around the world on:
www.111places.com

Foreword

The French Riviera, or Côte d'Azur, was one of the first regions in Europe to be both conquered and transformed by the tourism industry. The English founded the Promenade des Anglais, Cannes created its film festival, and St. Tropez invented a myth all its own. This does not mean, however, that this 125-mile stretch of coastline – or its hinterland reaching up into the Maritime Alps – is any less appealing to visitors today.

The French Riviera is a land steeped in history. Not only did the Romans leave their legacy, but there are also still traces of the Allied troops from World War II, who began the liberation of southern France here. The coastal strip also, of course, has immense cultural appeal: Nietzsche wrote his *Zarathustra* here, Jean Marais and Jean Cocteau left their marks, as did Le Corbusier and Eileen Gray.

The obligatory itinerary for any visitor to the Côte d'Azur will undoubtedly include the Royal Palace of Monaco, the Picasso Museum in Antibes, and the Fondation Maeght. But do you know about the Tibetan village stacked up one of the Riviera's hillsides? Are you familiar with the monument to the Belgian "Butcher of the Congo," Leopold II? Have you heard of the Buddhist pagoda in Fréjus? Do you know where to buy umbrellas in Nice or admire butterflies in St. Tropez?

This book will guide you through destinations on the French Riviera that will entice you with their charm and unusual character. It's a journey that will lead you to tattooed villas and whimsical tombs, along underwater paths, up escalators, and through mysterious covered walkways. The Côte d'Azur harbors many surprises – both great and small – many of which even the locals haven't discovered. One hundred and eleven temptations, including cultural highlights, hotel ruins, and remote mountain villages await you …

111 Places

1_ The Free Commune

Where boules is played with square balls

If you assumed the entire stretch of the Côte d'Azur belongs to the French state (except Monaco, of course), you would be wrong. There is one last region that has managed to withstand all invaders …

We are talking about the Commune Libre du Safranier in Antibes. This free commune was founded in the 1960s, not for political reasons, but to create a gathering place for festivals and to uphold the local traditions of the community. The "territory" of the municipality, led by an elected mayor-for-life, is limited to the neighborhood of the same name in the old town of Antibes, and extends between the Rue de la Tourraque and Rue du Haut Castellet. The Place du Safranier serves as its center, hidden behind ramparts only a stone's throw from the sea.

The narrow streets and lanes of the idyllic neighborhood are lined with charming houses that have facades covered with colorful flowers. Neighbors still chat with one another from their windows. Incidentally, the famous Greek writer Nikos Kazantzakis, who wrote *Zorba the Greek*, lived in the Safranier district after World War II. He spent the last years of his life occupying a little house on the Rue du Bas Castellet (number 8).

The activities of the commune still focus on the people of the community and their traditions. Numerous events are held throughout the year, such as the Feast of the Chestnuts and a festival celebrating the traditional *pistou* soup. The popular competition Bal National des Boules Carrées, where square boules balls get their day in the sun, takes place every year on July 14.

Since 1996, Zézé Marconi has served as the mayor, and he has often likened his experience here to that of the French cartoon character Obélix, with his magic potion: "I just fell into it when I was very young."

Address Place du Safranier, 06600 Antibes, www.communelibredusafranier.com | **Getting there** The Place du Safranier is located southwest of the old town. | **Tip** The Taverne du Safranier is a popular restaurant with a large outdoor terrace on the Place du Safranier. It is closed Monday and Sunday nights during the low season (Tel 0033/(0)493348050).

2__ The Nomade

Art at the marina

Antibes is home to both the famous Picasso Museum and the elegant Port Vauban. This yacht marina, named for master castle builder Sébastien le Prestre de Vauban, is not only – with its 2,000 moorings – the largest marina of the French Riviera, it is also the most glamorous because of the yachts at anchor along the quay. Even ships more than 165 feet long can easily find accommodation here in the harbor basin, and for this reason it's known as the *Quai des Milliardaires*. This is not an ironic nickname: even the *Kingdom KR5* and the *Carinthia VII*, famous yachts from the James Bond films, have docked here. Only Roman Abramovich can't find room at the marina: the Russian businessman's 535-foot yacht *Eclipse* must bob about in the bay.

While there are certainly those who consider stylish yachts to be works of art, at the Port Vauban you can also admire real art: since 2000, the sculpture *Nomade*, by the Catalan artist Jaume Plensa, has stood on the Bastion Saint-Jaume, a visual landmark that protrudes right out into the harbor. The 26-foot-high structure is made of thousands of white letters and depicts a person seated with his knees bent and his gaze turned toward the sea. With these luminous characters, the sculpture, which symbolizes the "soul of words," encourages viewers to think in new ways. Because *Nomade* is hollow, you can also easily see right through it, prompting unexpected views and new observations. Plensa's sculpture is particularly impressive when it is illuminated at night.

The Bastion Saint-Jaume is a part of the fortifications laid out by Vauban. Fort Carré at the north of the harbor is especially striking. With its star-shaped floor plan it is a classic example of 17th-century fortress architecture. Several bastions emanate from its round court-yard, which forms the center of the structure.

Address Bastion Saint-Jaume, 06600 Antibes | **Getting there** The Bastion Saint-Jaume is adjacent to the northeastern tip of the port. | **Hours** Tue – Sun 10am–8pm; in July and Aug, 10am–11pm | **Tip** Anyone interested in the art of Jaume Plensa can also see his seven sculptures on the Place Masséna in Nice.

3_ Villa Kérylos
Living in the past

Baron Théodore Reinach was an aesthete. This son of a wealthy Jewish banking family was a jurist and member of Parliament, but his real passions were archeology and classical studies. Reinach – who was related to the Rothschilds – fantasized about a life, and a villa, straight out of antiquity.

In Emmanuel Pontremoli, Reinach found an architect who shared his passion for the past, and without hesitation Pontremoli accepted the unusual contract to build a villa reminiscent of those from classical Greece. When Reinach finally acquired a suitable plot of land next to the sea in Beaulieu-sur-Mer, he fulfilled his lifelong dream with the construction of Villa Kérylos. This small palace was built between 1902 and 1908. It comprised 27,000 square feet, and its rooms were laid out, as in the ancient building tradition, around a central atrium (courtyard), along with the pergolas and patios typically found in such a home. Manor houses that had been excavated on the island of Delos served as inspiration for the villa.

Reinach's realization of the details was flawlessly authentic: the walls and floors were decorated with original frescoes and mosaics, and the rooms were appointed with fine custom-made reproductions of ancient furniture pieces. Even the textiles and household effects corresponded to historic models. Money was no object for Reinach: the bathroom, for example, was done entirely in fine Carrara marble. But Pontremoli was smart enough to hide all the plumbing inside the walls; although authenticity was important, Reinach did not want to sacrifice comfort and aesthetics to attain it.

Reinach used the Villa Kérylos as his summer residence until his death, in 1928. He willed the estate to the Institut de France, which is why visitors today can stroll through the villa and enjoy the unique atmosphere.

Address Impasse Gustave Eiffel, 06310 Beaulieu-sur-Mer, www.villa-kerylos.com | **Getting there** Beaulieu-sur-Mer is located 5 miles east of Nice on the M 6098. Impasse Gustave Eiffel is a small cul de sac, which branches off from the coastal road. | **Hours** July–Aug, daily 10am–7pm; Mar–June, Sep and Oct, daily 10am–6pm; Nov–Feb, Mon–Fri 2–6pm, Sat and Sun 10am–6pm | **Tip** From Beaulieu you can walk all the way to Saint-Jean-Cap-Ferrat directly along the coast on the Promenade Maurice Rouvier.

4_ Facade Advertisements

In search of forgotten brands

In terms of the relationship between marketing and consumption, France adopted the American advertising model early on. Huge super-markets can be found in every town, and cash registers with scanners have been a part of life in even the most remote mountain villages for well over two decades. What is sold must also be promoted, often annoyingly and aggressively on TV, radio, and billboards.

Compared with modern advertisements, you might view the historic ones you'll see on the walls of houses in Breil-sur-Roya with considerable goodwill. They are the nostalgically faded testimony of a simpler time in the world of consumer goods. After all, you can't paint a new design on the front of your house every week. As you walk through the streets, you're sure to discover a few of these *murs réclames*. Some facades were painted over several times, some have a bit of plaster crumbling, and some even have windows cut into the advertising space.

The *murs réclames* are an open-air museum of long-ago brands and products. Who today has ever heard of paint manufacturer Ripolin, Crème Éclipse cleanser, or the wine producers Pradel? Colorful signs on the houses appeared for the first time at the end of the 19th century, finding their heyday in the 1930s and 1950s. In addition to banks such as Crédit Lyonnais and newspapers like *Le Petit Marseillais*, alcohol brands such as Ricard and Suze were among those that mainly used this form of advertisement, and campaigns for aperitifs like Cinzano or Byrrh were particularly prolific.

The king of the *murs réclames* was Dubonnet, which always used the slogan *"Du bo, du bon, dubonnet,"* and a striking blue shade for their *vin tonique*. With the growth of modern media, however, companies began opting for new types of ads, and the bright facades of Breil-sur-Roya have all but faded away.

Address Boulevard Rouvier, 06540 Breil-sur-Roya | **Getting there** Breil-sur-Roya lies in the Roya Valley on the D 6204, about 19 miles north of Menton. | **Tip** In the nearby town of Tende, you can see a house facade painted with an advertisement for the gas station operator Azur.

5_ Train des Merveilles

A magical train trip

The Tenda Railway between France and Italy is one of the most beautiful train journeys in Europe. Spectacular bridge viaducts and tunnels are the trademarks of this line, which runs from Cuneo in Italy to Ventimiglia. A journey aboard is a thrill for anyone, not just train enthusiasts.

The first plans for a rail link from Piedmont to the Mediterranean already existed in 1851, when the entire Roya Valley was still part of Italy. But due to the difficult geographical conditions – it had to cover over 3,200 feet in altitude – and the complicated political situation at the time, the first trains didn't pass through the valley until October 1928. Simultaneously, a second, parallel line was opened, so that trains from Nice could run directly to Cuneo. The joint railway station between the two branches of the Tenda Railway was located in Breil-sur-Roya.

Breil-sur-Roya is a popular stop for those who ride the Train des Merveilles. This tourist train runs in the summer months between Nice and Tende, and its name alludes to the Vallée des Merveilles, or "Valley of Wonders," through which it passes. The region, part of the Mercantour National Park, is known for its prehistoric petro-glyphs, and at the end of the nearly 50-mile train ride there is a museum in Tende dedicated to them.

Depending on your level of desire, you can hop on and off the Train des Merveilles to explore any of the splendid Maritime Alps villages, such as Pillion or Sospel. Breil-sur-Roya itself is a lovely old town. In addition, the train travels through several different vegetation zones on the nearly two-hour trip. Palm trees and cypresses dominate in the first miles, but after a series of tunnel crossings, pine and spruce announce your arrival in the alpine mountain world, where the peaks are covered with snow even in the summertime.

Address Rue des Métiers, 06540 Breil-sur-Roya | **Getting there** Breil-sur-Roya lies in the Roya Valley on the D 6204 about 19 miles north of Menton. | **Hours** The train runs daily June–Sep, in May and Oct only on weekends | **Tip** The Ecomusée des Transports is located at the train station in Breil-sur-Roya, aptly dedicated to transportation. There are several historic buses and railway cars on display in its hall (May–Sep, daily 2–6pm, www.ecomusee-breil.com).

Train des merveilles

6 La Malmaison

An art gallery with a dark past

There is a pretty building on the famous Croisette promenade, a neoclassical mansion that is sure to catch your eye. On the square out front, palm trees line the pathway that leads up to the entry portal, which is flanked by columns. Aimé Maeght, who later founded the famous Fondation Maeght, organized his first exhibition of paintings on the French Riviera here. And since 1983, the city of Cannes has used the property for exhibitions of high-caliber modern art. From Matisse to Picasso, all the great modernists have been shown here.

But La Malmaison is more than just an art gallery; it is a building with an eventful history. Established in the 19th century as the tea-house and gaming parlor of the long demolished Grand Hôtel, the property was seized by Italian troops in November 1942. Until that month, the South of France had been a part of the unoccupied zone and had, for several years, served as a gathering point for rallies against political and ethnic persecution.

After the Allied forces reached North Africa, German and Italian soldiers marched into southern France, and the Italians occupied the border areas and established their headquarters in Cannes. For just under a year, they acted as occupiers, until the Germans came and took their place following Italy's surrender in September 1943. Immediately, the spiral of violence began to escalate. Raids and deportations of Jewish citizens were not the only item on the German agenda, but also the torture and execution of members of the French Resistance. Even as late as August 15, 1944 – the day the Allied troops landed on the coast of France – eight Resistance fighters, including one woman, were unceremoniously executed by the Gestapo in Cannes. Nine days later, Cannes was liberated, and the Germans took flight.

Address 47 Boulevard de la Croisette, 06400 Cannes | **Getting there** La Malmaison
is located directly on the Croisette. | **Hours** July–Sep, Tue–Sun 11am–8pm,
Fri 11am–10pm; Apr–June, 10am–1pm and 2:30–6:30pm; Oct–Mar, 10am–12pm and
2:30–6pm | **Tip** In front of the former Villa Montfleury, at Boulevard Montfleury 42,
a stone commemorates the "Victims of the Gestapo from August 15, 1944."

7__ The Lord Brougham Monument

The inventor of Cannes

You might think Cannes' success is due to its famous film festival. But it was actually Lord Brougham who was responsible for the city's rise from an insignificant fishing village in the early 19th century to what it has become today.

Ultimately, the city's transformation into a tourist metropolis came down to chance: in 1834, former British Chancellor of the Exchequer Lord Henry Brougham wanted to spend the winter in Nice – which at the time was still a part of Italy – with his ailing daughter, Eleanor, but there was a cholera epidemic in progress at the time and entry to the city was forbidden. Brougham was not allowed to cross the border at the River Var and had to remain in France. When the hotels in Antibes could not meet his needs, he discovered a suitable alternative accommodation in Cannes. He immediately fell in love with the charming locale, so much so that he decided not to continue on to Nice when the travel ban was lifted.

Brougham had a villa built in Cannes in the Italian style, on what is today the Avenue du Docteur-Picaud. He named it Château Eléonore-Louise. Thanks to his patronage, Cannes soon became one of the most exclusive destinations on the French Riviera. Brougham's influence was even felt by the French king, Louis-Philippe, who agreed to finance the construction of a new harbor in the town. In addition, Cannes received a railway connection, the famous promenade La Croisette was created, and the population quadrupled within a few decades.

After Lord Brougham died in his beloved Cannes on May 7, 1868, his friends commissioned the sculptor Paul Liénard to create a monument in his honor. It was unfortunately destroyed during World War II, but was replaced with a reproduction in 1952.

Address Allées de la Liberté Charles de Gaulle, 06400 Cannes | **Getting there** The memorial is a few hundred feet behind the Film Festival Palace. | **Tip** The monumental grave of Lord Brougham is located in the Cimetière du Grand Jas.

8__ The Curve
The fateful drive of Princess Grace

In 1982, the death of Princess Grace of Monaco shook the world in a way that can only be compared to the public's response to the untimely death of Britain's Princess Diana in 1997. Ever since Grace's fairy-tale wedding to Prince Rainier III, pictures and stories about the former American movie star had filled the tabloids every week. Her cool elegance was considered the ideal of beauty at the time. After filming the Alfred Hitchcock movie *To Catch a Thief* – in which the screen siren starred alongside Cary Grant – Grace Kelly was introduced to the Prince of Monaco at the film festival in nearby Cannes. A few weeks later, Rainier asked her to marry him over dinner at the Waldorf-Astoria Hotel in New York City.

Grace helped the principality ascend to an unimaginable level of glamor and was an extremely popular figure in the tiny country. On the morning of September 13, 1982, the princess was driving with her youngest daughter, Stéphanie, from the royal summer residence, Roc Agel, in the direction of Cap d'Ail from La Turbie, when she lost control of her vehicle on a hairpin turn. Her car tumbled more than 130 feet down a steep cliff. While Stéphanie, who, like her mother, was not wearing her seat belt, sustained only relatively minor injuries, Grace died a day later at the hospital in Monaco. She was buried with great sadness and emotion by a grieving nation.

What caused the tragic accident has remained a mystery to this day. One theory is that Princess Grace may have suffered a mild stroke while driving, while others suggest pills and alcohol might have been involved. In addition, there are persistent rumors that Princess Stéphanie, who was underage at the time, was actually the one behind the wheel of the Rover 3500, since witnesses saw her climb from the wreckage through the driver's door.

Address Route de la Turbie (43° 43' 35" N, 7° 24' 10" E), 06320 Cap d'Ail | **Getting there** Located between La Turbie and Cap d'Ail (D 37). | **Tip** Princess Grace's grave is located in the Cathédrale of Monaco. Her husband, Prince Rainier III, has rested at her side since April 2005.

9__ Plage Mala

An idyllic hidden beach

On the French Riviera, the beach is, quite simply, where it's at. It's the ultimate social stage where bathers come to see and be seen. This is true along the Côte d'Azur even more so than on Mallorca. Among the most popular beaches are the pebble beach in Nice, the backfilled city beach of Cannes, and the golden Plage de Pampelonne on the peninsula of St. Tropez – each one governed by its own set of social rules, unspoken but easily distinguished by those in the know.

Up and down the Mediterranean coast, the beaches are busy and crowded – especially in July and August – and in some places you'll be hard-pressed to even find enough room to lay down your towel. To make matters worse, the cliffs along the coast between Monaco and Beaulieu mean that there are only a few beaches accessible for bathing and tanning – which makes the hidden Plage Mala a particularly exciting find. Framed by rocky cliffs on the Cap d'Ail, it is rarely crowded even in the high season and offers magnificent natural scenery with shimmering crystal-clear turquoise water.

The Cap d'Ail, bordering the Principality of Monaco, has, since time immemorial, been one of the most upscale locations to live along the French Riviera. Winston Churchill and Greta Garbo, among others, have spent their vacations here. The Plage Mala benefits from this exquisite flair, because the beach lies at the foot of a posh neighborhood of villas where there is hardly any parking available, so the invasion of the masses is held at bay. Additionally, the beach is not easily accessible, since you have to descend a long flight of steps down to the water.

Once at the bottom, however, sun worshipers will find a true paradise with excellent diving, as well as two beachfront restaurants that pamper diners with superbly prepared fresh fish dishes.

Address Allée Mala, 06320 Cap d'Ail | **Getting there** Cap d'Ail is just over a mile west of Monaco on the coastal road (RN 98). The stairway to the beach begins at the end of the Allée Mala. | **Tip** It is worth taking a stroll through the Jardin Sacha Guitry, where you'll be inspired by the rich flora (87 Avenue du 3 Septembre).

10__ The World War II Landing Craft

Relic of Operation Dragoon

A gray landing craft stands alone on a huge parking lot not far from the Cap du Dramont. It is a reminder that things were not always so peaceful here along the coast of the Esterel Massif. When most people think about the arrival of the Allied troops during World War II, they automatically recall the battles on the beaches of Normandy; only a few are familiar with Operation Dragoon on the Côte d'Azur.

Two months after the invasion of Normandy began, in the early hours of August 15, 1944, Allied forces landed on a nearly 65-mile-long section of coastline, stretching from Le Lavandou in the west to the Esterel Massif in the east. A total of nearly 900 ships, 1,370 landing craft, 5,000 aircraft, and nearly 200,000 soldiers were involved in Operation Dragoon. After a fierce air raid on the German positions, several thousand parachutists floated through the darkness to touch down behind enemy lines. The sky was cloudy when the first soldiers landed on the beach at around 8 o'clock in the morning. The attacks were concentrated on several strategic coastal sections, with the Cap du Dramont one of the most hotly contested areas. The soldiers of the 36th US Infantry Division from Texas actually wanted to conquer the Cap Anthéor, but due to the fierce resistance from the troops there, switched their efforts instead to the Cap du Dramont, where the opposition was notably weaker.

Operation Dragoon was a great success. The German troops could not withstand the attack for long. Within a few weeks, their defensive lines broke down, and Allied forces advanced over the Rhone Valley to the north. Today, the anniversary of the landing is still celebrated by the residents of Cap du Dramont, as well as by those in other participating villages and towns.

Address Cap du Dramont, 83700 Le Dramont | **Getting there** The landing craft stands on the Cap du Dramont very close to the coastal road (D 559). | **Tip** The hour-long coastal walk around the Cap du Dramont is breathtaking.

11_Musée de la Mine

In the realm of minerals

A mine on the French Riviera's beautiful coast? At first, the idea seems downright unthinkable. Normally, all one expects to see along the waterfront in the South of France are stately villas. But as you drive the road between Toulon and Hyères-Plage, you'll find yourself alongside a former lead and copper mine lying hidden on the Cap Garonne. It originally began operations in 1862, and, since there was a lack of skilled labor in France, most of the miners who worked there came from the Italian region of Piedmont. As was customary at the time, women and children were also employed in the arduous work.

Since the copper content of the ore was too low to generate large profits, the mine changed hands several times. Despite repeated expansion of the railway network, the operation was eventually no longer profitable, and eventually closed down in October 1917.

It was only in the 1970s that about 100 rare mineral species and crystals were found in the humid climate of the abandoned mine, which roused not only the interest of scientists, but also looters. In order to put a stop to the thievery and protect the extraordinary mineral wealth of the site, a decision was made to establish a museum in the tunnels. It was not until 1994, however, that the Musée de la Mine finally opened.

The Musée de la Mine is considered one of the most beautiful mineral museums in France. Equipped with hard hats, visitors can explore the former mine on a guided tour and get a feel for this fascinating underground world. You can admire the extraordinary mineral collection as you walk through, but also, with the help of sound effects and videos, gain insights into the workings and conditions of the former copper mine and the processing of the precious raw materials.

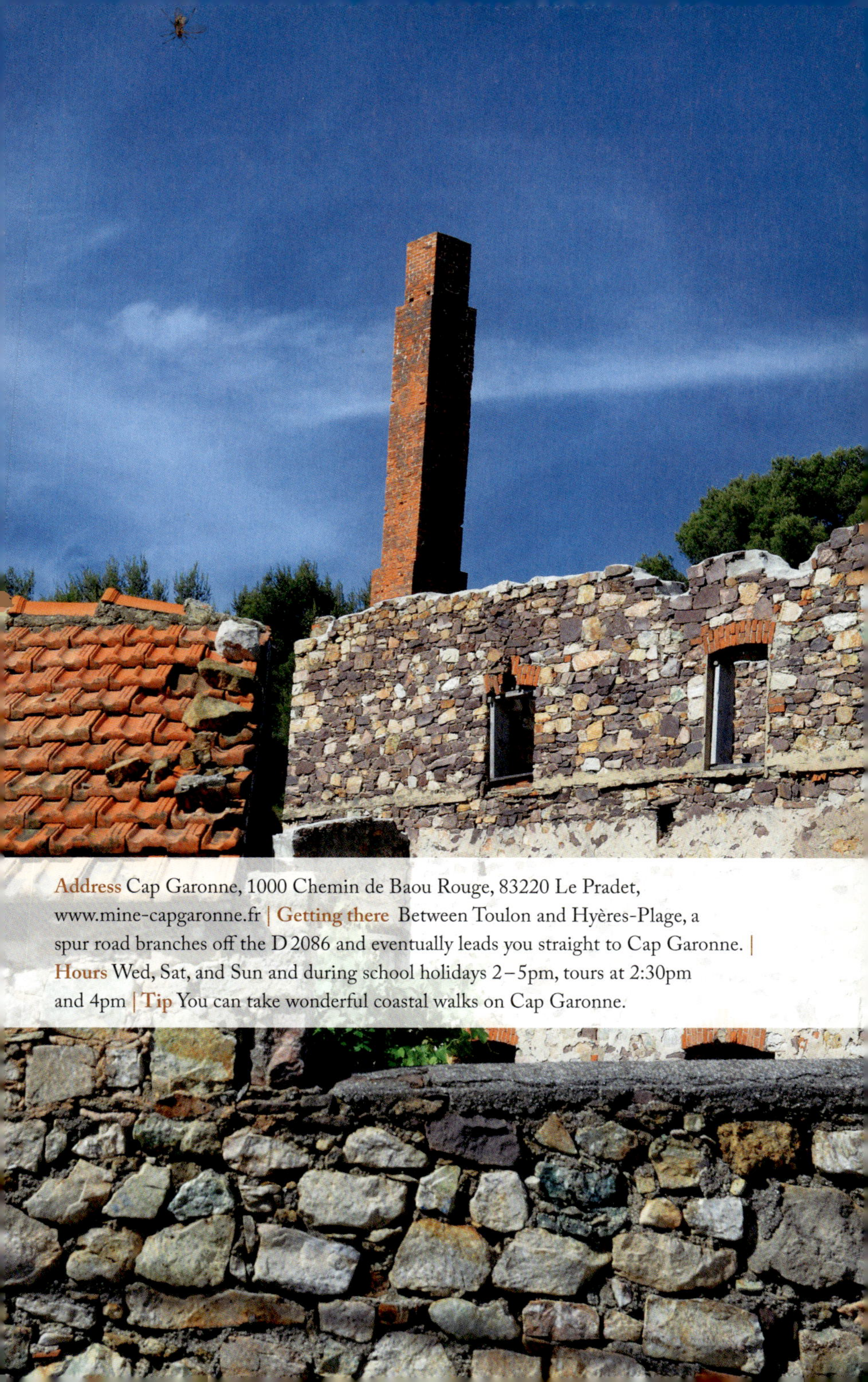

Address Cap Garonne, 1000 Chemin de Baou Rouge, 83220 Le Pradet, www.mine-capgaronne.fr | **Getting there** Between Toulon and Hyères-Plage, a spur road branches off the D 2086 and eventually leads you straight to Cap Garonne. | **Hours** Wed, Sat, and Sun and during school holidays 2–5pm, tours at 2:30pm and 4pm | **Tip** You can take wonderful coastal walks on Cap Garonne.

12__The Village of Sundials

Art in the sign of the sun

The hinterland of the French Riviera gets as much sun as the coastline, and the olives that ripen on the slopes and in the valleys here are popular due to their intense, mildly spicy flavor. The road that stretches up from Contes to the Col St-Roch makes for a lovely drive since it is typically drenched in sunlight. Directly on this *Route du Soleil* lies Coaraze, a village with lots of medieval charm and vaulted passages. With so many hours of sunshine a year, it is no surprise that, from time immemorial, when men in Coaraze wanted to know what hour it was, they just turned their heads toward the sun.

Around the middle of the 20th century, Coaraze, like many other similar villages, began struggling with the exodus of its people to the cities. Because of this, in 1961, mayor Paul Mari d'Antoine came up with the idea of inviting renowned artists to create sundials in any style and manner that they wished in his village. Since then, the walls of the forecourt of the church and the facades of the local post office and town hall have been decorated with several handsome ceramic sundials, which further testify to Coaraze's reputation as a village known for its art and handicrafts.

The best-known artist to take part in this project was certainly Jean Cocteau. The Renaissance man designed his sundial with images of lizards. Georges Douking used mythical creatures, the famous ceramic artist Gilbert Valentin employed an ornate sunflower motif, and other decorative timepieces were made by Henri Bernard Goetz and Angelo Ponce de Leon.

In 2008, the village decided to revive the initiative. Once again, renowned contemporary artists such as Sacha Sosno, Fabienne Barre, Patrick Moya, and Henri Macheroni were invited to Coaraze to design ceramic sundials, and there are now 11 pieces on public display.

Ponce de Léon

Address 06043 Coaraze | **Getting there** From Nice, take the D 15 north. | **Tip** The artist Angelo Ponce de Léon not only designed a sundial, but, in 1962, he also decorated the Chapelle Notre-Dame-des-Sept-Douleurs with colorful blue frescoes. Since then, it is also known as the "*chapelle bleue*" (key available at the bar in the village).

13_Les Pipes de Cogolin
Home of the pipe carvers

It's not just the pipe smokers of the world whose eyes widen when they hear the name Cogolin. The small town on the edge of the Massif des Maures has a grand tradition of craftsmanship. Furniture and handspun carpets from Cogolin can be found in the Palace of Versailles as well as in the White House. The natural cork found here also commands top prices and the raw materials used in the production of high-quality bottle corks are still harvested from the numerous cork oak groves in the hinterland.

Along with cork, the raw materials used to make the famous pipes of Cogolin are also found in the forests of the Massif des Maures. The famous Bruyere pipes are crafted from the knotted roots of the briars that grow here. The root timber of the *Erica arborea* is not only beautifully textured, but also resistant to heat, allowing the tobacco smoke to develop evenly. Pipe smokers often appreciate the slight honey aftertaste produced by the pipes.

Cogolin's pipes are inextricably linked to the name Courrieu. The family enterprise was founded back in 1802. Since then, the art of making pipes has been passed down from generation to generation. Courrieu's customers have included pipe lovers such as the writer Georges Simeon and the politician Edgar Faure. Currently, the business is run by René Courrieu and his son Thierry, who care passionately about traditional forms of production. In their studio, visitors receive a detailed explanation of the various stages of the manufacturing process. A great deal of expertise is needed to produce one of these ornate pipes. It's no wonder that the most beautiful ones can cost upwards of 200 euros, but not to worry, there are much more affordable pipes available as well. If you like, you can also bring your favorite pipe with you and have it repaired on-site.

Address 42 Avenue Georges Clemenceau, 83310 Cogolin, www.courrieupipes.fr | **Getting there** Cogolin is located about 6 miles west of St. Tropez on the D98, which you exit at the first roundabout in the direction of *"Centre ville."* | **Hours** Studio: Mon–Sat 9am–12pm and 2–6pm; Shop: 9am–7pm | **Tip** For those who find carpets more interesting than pipes, there is the Manufacture de Tapis in Cogolin at 6 Boulevard Louis-Blanc (www.manufacturecogolin.com).

14_ Chartreuse de la Verne

Praying in the solitude of the Massif des Maures

The Massif des Maures is a lonely and inhospitable place. Until you get to Collobrières, there aren't any towns or villages, and only rarely will you catch a glimpse of a solitary farmstead peeking out from the forests and thick vegetation. Maouro, from which the Massif draws its name, was the old Provençal term for a dark, barely accessible forest.

In other words, this is the perfect place for a monastery. Here, in the solitude of the Massif, there are no threats of distraction, and only the chirping of the cicadas might interrupt the contemplation of God. The Carthusians established a monastery here on a small plateau in 1170, and soon, with the help of numerous donations, it was expanded over a large swath of land. The buildings were damaged or destroyed several times over the centuries by both forest fires and looting, but the monks rebuilt the monastery repeatedly and erected great retaining walls. The present state of the charterhouse largely corresponds to what existed during the 17th and 18th centuries.

The revolution of 1789 put an abrupt end to the idyll. The monastery was secularized, and its rich furnishings sold and scattered. Although the ruins were declared a historical monument in 1921, its decline continued. Only after 1982, when the religious community of the Sisters of Bethlehem took up residence here, did things start to turn around. Since then, the secluded monastery has been filled once again with religious life – 30 nuns currently occupy the old building – and much-needed restoration work has begun. In the publicly accessible parts of the complex, you can visit a historic oil press, a bakery, and the refurbished charterhouse, where the monastery cemetery, with its simple wooden crosses and two cloisters, is especially impressive.

Address 83610 Collobrières | **Getting there** From Collobrières, the little D 14 leads in the direction of Grimaud. After a few miles, a spur road branches off to the right leading to the Chartreuse. | **Hours** June–Aug, Mon, Wed–Sun 11am–6pm; Sep–Dec and Feb–May, Mon, Wed–Sun 11am–5pm; closed Easter, Pentecost, and Christmas, as well as the month of January and August 15th | **Tip** From La Môle, you can also walk to the charterhouse by the Barrage de la Verne (a reservoir) in about three hours.

15_ Confiserie Azuréenne

In chestnut heaven

The Massif des Maures is a fascinating mountain range due to its isolation in the hinterland of St. Tropez. In case you were wondering, its name derives from the Provençal word *Maouro*, an old designation for a dark, barely accessible forest, which in this case is made up of chestnuts, cork oaks, and Aleppo pines. For a long time, the Massif des Maures was only reachable by mule tracks, so most residents led a rather simple life. In addition to cork production and beekeeping, the processing of chestnuts was the primary way for locals to eke out a living.

Chestnuts, with their sweet, nutty flavor, can be used in many ways: they can be ground into flour for baking, and their leaves and shells can be given to cattle as feed, while the wood can be used in the construction of houses and furniture. Even today, approximately 600 tons are harvested a year.

Located in a narrow valley, Collobrières is the capital of the Massif des Maures. Although the community has only 1,800 residents, it has served a central function for centuries in this sparsely populated area, which is why its handsome marketplace is still thriving.

For those who love chestnuts, a visit to the Confiserie Azuréenne in Collobrières is a must. It's considered the best place in the region to satiate your hankering for candied chestnuts, purée, and jam. In the attached store, there are a wide variety of other chestnut products, such as nougat or liqueur. In the summer, you will understand what all the fuss is about when you have your first taste of the delicious chestnut ice cream flavored with cognac. There is also a small museum connected to the Confiserie, which lovingly tells of the local chestnut cultivation, and displays numerous historical production devices. An annual chestnut festival takes place in Collobrières on the last three Sundays in October.

Address Boulevard Koenig, 83610 Collobrières, www.confiserieazureenne.com | **Getting there** Collobrières is located on the D 14, about 21 miles north of Le Lavendou; the Boulevard Koenig branches off from the D 14 in town. | **Hours** Daily 9:30am–12:30pm and 1:30–7:30pm | **Tip** On Sunday mornings, there is a large market where you can pick up some chestnut puree.

16__Dolmen Pierre de la Fée

Even ancient man was drawn to the French Riviera

The lovely stretch of coast between Menton and St. Tropez and the inland area behind it must have exerted a certain magnetism even in ancient times – after all, this region boasts one of the oldest continuous settlements in human history. Early signs of humanity on the French Riviera have been discovered, for example, in a cave known as the Grotte du Lazaret on Mount Boron in Nice. Remains such as these, as well as some two dozen menhirs (stone monoliths) and dolmens (tombs that resemble a table made of large, mostly unhewn stone blocks), under which many skeletons were found, are evidence of early civilization. These monuments were built with great effort in the period between 6500 and 2000 BC by the local population.

You can find dolmen tombs in Ramatuelle (Dolmen de la Briande) and in Ampus (Dolmen de Marenc), but the largest and most imposing of all is the Dolmen Pierre de la Fée, which stands in the outskirts of Draguignan. This monumental rebuilt gravesite consists of three pedestal stones more than six feet tall, upon which rests an 18-foot-long and nearly 15-foot-wide stone plate that weighs more than 20 tons. During excavations, several skeletons were discovered, along with sacrificial burial offerings such as flint tools and beaded jewelry.

A legend has grown up around the dolmen. The fairy Estérelle, disguised as a shepherdess, promised her lover she would marry him if he would build a huge stone table for her, but he was too weak to heave the tabletop onto the legs, so the fairy conjured up the massive stone herself.

On January 28, 1975, the dolmen almost fell victim to an attack. Political activists, protesting the fact that Draguignan had been downgraded to a sub-prefecture of the Département of Var, detonated an explosive device at the base of the stone monument.

Address Avenue de Montferrat, 83300 Draguignan | **Getting there** Northwest of Draguignan, Avenue de Montferrat branches eastward from the D 2955 in La Louve. | **Tip** The Dolmen de Peicervier stands in the Hameau Sainte-Jaume district of nearby Lorgues (about 9 miles south).

17_The Mysterious House Facade

Who really was Claude Gay?

The wide boulevards of Paris are integral to the city's life and charm, and strolling along them is a favorite activity of tourists and locals alike. But Paris isn't the only place in France with wide avenues and boulevards. You can also find them in the Provençal town of Draguignan. You might assume they were modeled after Paris's design, but you'd be mistaken, since the broad streets of Draguignan came first. In fact, Baron Georges-Eugène Haussmann, known as the "inventor of the boulevards of Paris," served as the prefect of Draguignan in 1849, when it was still the capital of the Département of Var. Just four years later the agile administrator was commissioned by Napoleon III to tackle the redesign of Paris.

As you stroll the boulevards of Draguignan today, you'll come upon a huge stylized portrait adorning a strikingly painted facade. Over the only window on the facade, there are painted the words: *Claude Gay – un explorateur et savant provençal au chili.* Claude *who*?

Claude Gay was a contemporary of Baron Haussmann. But instead of boulevards, Gay, who was born in Draguignan in 1800, was more interested in botany. As a naturalist, he undertook extensive research trips to South America, where he lived for decades under government contract in Chile and studied the world of nature and plants. He was the first European to point out the healing power of the maqui berry, whose juice was drunk by the Mapuche Indians.

Gay's most important work is considered to be the *Historia Física y Política de Chile*, which includes detailed descriptions of local Chilean customs and an exhaustive *Botánica*, which describes the flora of the country. Gay later returned to Provence and died not far from Flayosc, in 1873.

Address Place Claude Gay (Boulevard de la Liberté/corner of Rue Jean Aicard), 83300 Draguignan | **Getting there** Draguignan is located about 30 miles north of St. Tropez. | **Tip** An interesting agricultural collection is displayed in the Musée des Arts et Traditions Populaires de Moyenne Provence located at 15 Rue Roumanille (Tue–Sat 9am–12pm and 2–6pm; in summer also Sun 2–6pm).

18 The Rhône American Cemetery

Memorializing 861 heroes

The landing of Allied troops on the beaches of Normandy and on France's Mediterranean coast were both strategically important events that directly helped usher in the end of the National Socialist domination of Europe during World War II. In contrast to Operation Overlord in Normandy, however, Operation Dragoon is now largely forgotten by most people, although the landing of Allied forces on the Mediterranean was critical to the liberation of southern France. On the first day of the invasion, August 15, 1944, nearly 100,000 soldiers and around 11,000 vehicles came ashore. Within four weeks, the US Army, fighting together with French Resistance soldiers, had penetrated deeply into the Rhone valley as far as Dijon, although they suffered heavy losses along the way.

The Rhône American Cemetery and Memorial in Draguignan is not quite as monumental as the famous American military cemetery in Normandy at Colleville, but the graves here are still an impressive reminder of the high death toll American troops suffered during Operation Dragoon.

Eight hundred and thirty-seven white marble crosses and 24 Stars of David, aligned in geometric rows on the evergreen grass carpet, quietly admonish visitors of the cost of the war. They memorialize the dead, among whom, for example, is Private First Class Lattie Tipton, the first American soldier killed on the morning of August 15. On the Wall of the Missing, the names of another 294 soldiers who went MIA are engraved.

At the 30-acre site, you'll also be able to visit the nearly 70-foot-high monument and memorial chapel, as well as a visitor's center and a bronze relief that depicts the advance of the Allied troops and the liberation of the South of France.

Address 553 Boulevard John Kennedy, 83300 Draguignan | **Getting there** Draguignan is located about 30 miles north of St. Tropez, and the cemetery is on the D 59 about a quarter mile southeast of the town center. | **Hours** Daily 9am–5pm | **Tip** In Toulon, the Mémorial du Débarquement en Provence honors the landing of the Allies at Mont Faron.

19_ The Fortified Town
A bulwark in the Maritime Alps

Although Entrevaux, which means "between the valleys," was by late antiquity already settled and even an episcopal see, the town today is known above all for its powerful citadel, which is perched atop a rocky outcropping over the fortified town. The fortress is connected to the village by a steep, walled access road. Viewed together, the fortifications can truly be considered a work of art.

In 1693, in the wake of French clashes with the Duke of Savoy, Sébastien le Prestre de Vauban (1633–1707) built the border fortifications in this strategically important location. As the military architect of the "Sun King," Louis XIV, Vauban built more than 300 defense systems to secure the borders of the French kingdom. But he was known not just for the sheer number of military structures he completed, but also because he was a master of esthetics and site planning, designing defensive structures of architectural value and integrating them into their scenic locales and terrain. This is all the more remarkable when you consider that Vauban usually planned and monitored his construction projects from far away, using only maps and written descriptions.

During World War I, the fortress in Entrevaux was actually turned into a prisoner-of-war camp for German officers. Today, you can still pass through the mighty town gate flanked by towers in Entrevaux, which was built directly on the right bank of the Var River. The historic town center consists of only a few dozen houses packed closely together and enclosed by a ring of fortified walls. Even the former cathedral is integrated into the wall, an ancient custom that has not found its way into modern construction. To get the quintessential photo of Entrevaux, climb the hill opposite the town; from there you'll capture the whole town in a panoramic view.

Address 04320 Entrevaux | **Getting there** Entrevaux lies in the Var Valley on the D 4202. It is about 55 miles from Nice. | **Hours** Daily 9am–7pm | **Tip** In the Musée de la Moto, in the middle of the village, there is a collection of 75 historic motorcycles (May–Sep, daily 10am–12pm and 2–6pm).

20__ The Aqueduct
Water to the mills

Nearly every kid in Europe knows about the famous Pont du Gard, but the Roman aqueduct in Fayence is barely common knowledge to local historians. Admittedly, compared to the Pont du Gard, the Fayence aqueduct looks a little puny, and it only dates from late antiquity, making it three or four centuries younger than the Pont du Gard. Nevertheless, it is an impressive monumental structure that bears witness to the great technical capability of ancient Roman engineers.

As part of the Roman Empire, the Côte d'Azur and its hinterland were provided with excellent infrastructure, including roads, bridges, and even aqueducts, because not only did the Romans love their baths, but they also required sufficient water for their fields and the operation of grist mills. The aqueduct of Fayence was needed to process grains. The water was brought in along an artificial route from the foothills of the southern Alps to set the mighty mill in motion. Years later, however, Roman architecture was not held in such high regard, and planners had the nerve to lay a road right through the middle of the aqueduct.

The town of Fayence was first mentioned in print in the 12th century as *Favienta Loca*, or "advantageous place," and shortly afterward the bishop of Fréjus built a summer residence here. Today Fayence is a quaint old village harboring a variety of restaurants, hotels, and artisanal shops, with its steep lanes and houses leading upward to the ruins of the castle.

It turns out that one of the buildings, the Moulin de la Camandoule, was built in 1834 on the foundations of a 15th-century Roman mill. In 1968, it was converted into a posh country hotel with a large park and grounds. When the builders began digging to install a swimming pool for guests, they unearthed Roman bricks and other ancient relics.

Address Chemin de Notre-Dame des Cyprès, 83440 Fayence | **Getting there** Reached via the D19 about a half mile southwest of the village. | **Tip** The Moulin de la Camandoule is a wonderful country inn with an excellent restaurant (Tel 0033/(0)494760084, www.camandoule.com).

21__ The Baptistery

One of the oldest Christian buildings in France

Fréjus is known today for its wide sandy beaches and its many campgrounds. But most tourists are only marginally aware of the city's rich cultural heritage. Ever since Caesar chose this spot to settle the veterans of his 8th Legion, this city sitting at the mouth of the River Argens has been continuously inhabited.

A truly historic artistic jewel in Fréjus is the baptistery, built at the turn of the 6th century AD in the shape of a Greek cross. After the baptistery of Poitiers, it is one of the oldest religious buildings in all of France. This is not altogether surprising, given that Fréjus had already been raised to a bishopric seat in the year 374, and played an important role in the Christianization of the country.

The first view of the baptistery can be seen through a grate to the left of the entrance to the cathedral. The care with which the construction of this baptistery was undertaken reflects the importance the Christian community of the time ascribed to this sacramental rite of passage. The baptistery was deliberately placed in a separate building outside the actual cathedral, since no one who hadn't been baptized was allowed to enter the church itself.

Typical of construction in late antiquity are the octagonal upper floor and the high tambour, an architectural element connecting the building to its dome, which owes its name to its drum-shaped appearance. Along the side walls, semicircular and rectangular niches alternate, and between them rise monolithic pillars of gray marble crowned with white marble capitals, which all originated from older Roman buildings.

Right in the middle of the rotunda is the baptismal font, which was embedded in the ground so that the person being baptized experienced quite a dip. Another smaller basin was used to clean the feet prior to baptism.

Address Place Camile Formigé, 83600 Fréjus | **Getting there** Fréjus is located between Cannes and St. Tropez on the coastal road D 559. | **Hours** Daily 9am–6:30pm; Oct–Sep, 9am–12pm and 2–5pm | **Tip** The two-story cloister of the cathedral, with both its rounded Romanesque and pointed Gothic arches, is also worth a visit.

22 — Étangs de Villepey

Skinny-dipping in paradise

Unspoiled pristine coastlines are rare on the French Riviera. Real-estate prices are high, and the region is one of the most densely populated areas in France. Between Menton and St. Tropez, there are only a few large areas that have remained untouched by civilization, such as the Étangs de Villepey. This fascinating marshy landscape, fed by both salt water and fresh water from the Argens delta, reaches out into the sea much as the famous Camargue region further up the coast does. It was designated a nature reserve in 1982.

The nearly 650 acres of the site have an extraordinary collection of flora and fauna. Botanists delight in the extensive marshes full of reeds and salicornia, but also in rarer plant species such as samphire and orchids, including *Serapias*. In the brackish water zone, more than 200 species of birds breed in the springtime, including pink flamingos, silver and gray herons, European bee-eaters, little bitterns, corn buntings, and reed warblers. In the Étangs, both freshwater and saltwater fish thrive, and between the rushes hide smallmouth bass, smelt, mullet, and carp. It is more difficult for visitors to come face-to-face with the park's more reticent residents, such as the mud turtles or raccoons, since guests are required to stay on designated nature trails while roaming the nature preserve.

The Étangs de Villepey lies directly on the Mediterranean. A stretch of beach more than a mile long extends behind the dunes west of the small river Argens, which is arguably one of the most beautiful beaches of the French Riviera, with its coarse-grained sand and excellent water quality. You won't find any bars or bath-houses with beach umbrellas here though, and skinny-dipping is often reported at the less crowded area of the beach's easternmost section, at the river's mouth.

Address 83600 Fréjus | **Getting there** Between Fréjus and Saint-Aygulf on the coastal road (D 559). The entrance to the parking lot, which charges a fee in high summer, is about a half mile past the campsite, La Plage d'Argens, on the left-hand side. From there it is only a few hundred yards by foot down to the sea. | **Tip** Buses run from the center of Fréjus to the nature preserve.

23__ The Pagoda

A Buddhist temple on the Riviera

A Buddhist sanctuary on the Côte d'Azur? Surprising perhaps, but true nonetheless. The hipped roof of a real pagoda rises elegantly over a small hill here in Fréjus. The presence of this unusual cultural artifact is ultimately due to France's imperialist past.

The garrison town of Fréjus was an important hub for the colonial troops from Africa and Asia who fought on the side of their mother country in World War I, and many left behind traces of their cultures when they passed through. So in Fréjus you'll find not only a church modeled on one of the famous Missiri mosques in Mali, but also a Buddhist pagoda, built in 1917 by soldiers of the 4th infantry regiment, who originated in Indochina.

After the end of World War I, the Hông Hiên-Tu pagoda was abandoned and fell into disrepair. Then, in 1954, Vietnamese refugees who had resettled in Fréjus renovated the building and once again undertook their Buddhist worship here. Today, the temple building on a square base is modeled on the traditional Vietnamese style and is surrounded by expansive gardens, which now also play host to a Taoist temple.

During a stroll through the gardens, you can admire the exotic flora, such as lotus flowers, and enjoy numerous Buddha statues and colorful groups of figures, including dragons, elephants, and horses, all of which are believed to play curative or protective roles. With a length of nearly 33 feet, the sleeping Buddha of Fréjus is considered the largest in Europe. The great bell, weighing two tons, is also an impressive sight.

French Buddhists still meet every year in Fréjus to celebrate their most important holidays together in the pagoda. The garden is open to the public, but access to the pagoda is reserved for Buddhists only.

Address 13 Rue Henri Giraud, 83608 Fréjus | **Getting there** The DN 7 leads directly to the center of town. From there, continue just over a mile toward Cannes to the roundabout where the D 37 branches off. | **Hours** May–Sep, daily 9am–9pm; Oct–Apr, daily 9am–6pm; Tai Chi Chuan: Sun 10:30am, Qi Gong: Sun 11am | **Tip** In the same neighborhood stands the Mémorial des Guerres en Indochine, commemorating the 24,000 French soldiers and civilians who were killed during the Indochina Wars.

24__Gorges de Daluis
A canyon paradise

The canyon landscapes of the South of France have a magical attraction for motorcyclists. You'd be hard-pressed to pass through a rocky gorge without at some point seeing a few bikers casually managing the bends in the road. Among the most popular of these canyons is the Gorges de Daluis, which was carved into the rocky landscape by the flow of the Var River.

A road runs through the dazzling reddish rock of the gorge, leading from the village of Guillaumes southward to the eponymous town of Daluis, where it joins the larger D 6202. For much of the ride, the winding road runs through narrow passages right alongside the Var, and, in parts, also climbs high above the river. Take the time to stop often at the roadside pull-offs, because the views are stunning, not only of the surrounding mountain peaks, but also of the small streams that fall majestically into the canyon as waterfalls.

Equally impressive as the Gorges de Daluis is the nearby Gorges Supérieures du Cians,which lies in a valley to the east. Navigating through a series of tunnels and steep rocky overhangs, the sky is often visible only as a narrow blue ribbon. The vegetation also changes completely within a short distance, because the small river Cians covers more than 3,200 feet in height during its run. In two places, Petit Clue and Grand Clue, you can stop and walk along a small stretch of the raging river.

You can easily see both canyons together on a roughly 50-mile circular route that also takes you through Valberg, Guillaumes, Entrevaux, and Puget-Théniers. Valberg is one of the most famous winter sports resorts in the French Maritime Alps. At an altitude of more than 5,200 feet, good snow conditions are guaranteed far into the spring. And from Nice, it's a straight shot, just an hour and a half by car.

Address Gorges de Daluis | **Getting there** The Gorges de Daluis is about 60 miles
northwest of Nice. The D 2202 runs through the entire canyon. | **Tip** In the summer,
daring bungee jumpers plunge almost 275 feet from the Pont de la Mariêe, an impressive
arch bridge.

25_ The Eagle's Nest

Hike to a grand view

There are at least two dozen places in the hinterland of the French Riviera that vie for the unofficial title of "most spectacularly situated mountain village." Those serving on the fictional jury would certainly reserve a place on the podium for Gourdon, a mountain village steeped in history in an incomparable setting.

If you drive on the winding Route de Caussols northward from Grasse, an impressive mountain panorama opens up before you: Gourdon, clinging to a cliff nearly 2,500 feet above the valley – or rather, the canyon of the Loup River – seems just like an aerie, or *nid d'aigle* ("eagle's nest"). An even better way to take in the view, however, is on the two-hour hike up the canyon from Bar-sur-Loup on the Chemin du Paradis. In ever-increasing curves, the heavenly path winds itself up to Gourdon on the Aqueduct du Foulon. It is a truly impressive sight. Whether the mailmen who had to trudge up this route once a day well into the 20th century also felt this way, though, is more difficult to say.

Gourdon itself is a village whose residents never had to worry much about security. On the valley side, it is impregnable, and a mighty castle protects the northern entrance to the village. This castle, called the Château de Gourdon, was rebuilt and expanded in the 17th century in the Renaissance style. None other than André Le Nôtre, the famous landscape architect of Versailles, designed the formal terraced gardens with box trees and myrtle bushes manicured into spherical and cylindrical shapes. Visits are only available for groups by appointment.

The cobbled streets of the village, on the other hand, from which traffic was banished long ago, are freely accessible to all. While strolling through the village, though, be sure to keep your eyes trained on the grand views of the coast instead of the souvenir shops.

Address 06620 Gourdon, www.chateau-gourdon.com | **Getting there** Gourdon is located 25 miles north of Cannes, right on the D 12. | **Tip** Farther north lies the plateau of Caussols, a barren, uninhabited limestone plateau with almost surreal rock formations.

26_ The Perfumer
The fragrance vendor's tray

Grasse is known as the capital of fragrances and perfumes. Located in the hinterland of the Côte d'Azur, the village's reputation is originally due to the tannery that was located here. As scented leather gloves became popular in the European courts of the 16th century, the fragrance industry exploded in Grasse, which has a microclimate highly conducive to the cultivation of flora used to make perfume. More recently, the town has once again become known the world over thanks to Patrick Süskind's mega best seller, *Perfume: The Story of a Murderer.*

Busloads of visitors arrive here daily, carting people to major perfumer Galimard and Fragonard to stock up on the latest fragrances. Visitors pay little attention, however, to the three-foot-tall bronze sculpture of a medieval perfumer by Polish-born artist Tomek Kawiak.

Back in 1997, Kawiak did not get the idea for the sculpture purely from his imagination; he used the late-17th-century copper engraving *Habit de Parfumeur*, by Nicolas de Larmessin, as his model. De Larmessin created a series of 97 engravings depicting craftsmen and traders in peculiar costumes. In the presentation of his perfume merchant, de Larmessin became a bizarre sort of fashion designer, dressing him in a jacket with ladies' fans as epaulets and placing a distillation pot on his head. He also wears a vendor's tray with aromatic essences in filled bottles, such as malt and eaux d'ange, as well as lozenges and salves. Around his waist dangle small sacks of herbs, cedarwood, cire d'Espagne, rouge d'Espagne, and tobacco, and he holds scented towels and balls in his hands.

The statue depicts a time long before our modern temples of perfumery, but even back then, people paid a pretty penny for their beloved essences.

Address Boulevard Fragonard, 06130 Grasse | **Getting there** Grasse is located 12.5 miles northwest of Cannes and is reached quickly via the D 6185. When you reach the town, turn right onto the D 2562, then park in the nearby garage under the Place du Cours Honoré-Cresp. | **Tip** The neighboring perfume museum is especially interesting (8 Place du Cours Honoré Cresp, Apr – Sep, daily 10am – 7pm; Oct – Mar, Mon, Wed – Sun 10:30am – 5:30pm, closed holidays and 3 weeks in Nov, www.museesdegrasse.com).

27_Castel Pierre Lisse

Spend the night among works of modern art

For quite some time now, *chambres d'hôtes* have replaced the hotels and campgrounds on the French Riviera as the most popular places to spend the night. Don't think of this prevalent French version of a bed and breakfast as merely some sparse guest rooms with simple and boring furnishings, however, but instead as rural properties, and occasionally also beautiful city palaces or castles, where one or more rooms are rented to overnight visitors. The law only stipulates that no more than five rooms may be rented to up to 15 people, and that the landlord must dwell in the same or an adjacent building.

Castel Pierre Lisse, one of the most beautiful and unusual *chambres d'hôtes* on the Côte d'Azur, sits on the edge of the old town of Hyères. The stately 19th-century property not only affords magnificent coastal views, but also delights guests with its fascinating furnishings. There are so many works of art and photography displayed around the house and garden that you'll feel like you're living in a gallery of contemporary art; in one corner stands a small sculpture by Niki de Saint Phalle, in another is a vase by Jean Cocteau. There is no question: the owner, Nicolas, is an avid art collector and an equally attentive host.

All five guest rooms and the common areas are lovingly decorated with vintage furniture, including many classic pieces by renowned designers such as Le Corbusier and Arne Jacobsen. In the "Chambre Jade," for example, you'll find lamps by Ingo Maurer and a chair by Verner Panton.

Fortunately, there's no need to sacrifice comfort for style, as the spacious rooms and their magnificent bathrooms are on a par with that of any luxury hotel. Guests can relax in the beautiful garden or by the private pool, where dinner will happily be served upon request.

Address 1 Rue du Château, 83400 Hyères, Tel 0033/(0)494311118, www.castel-pierre-lisse.com |
Getting there Hyères is located 12.5 miles east of Toulon, at the end of the A 570 highway. |
Tip The Villa Noailles in Hyères has an inspiring cubist garden and is used for exhibitions and
fashion shows (www.villanoailles-hyeres.com).

28__ The Old Saltworks

A nature reserve in the salt marshes

The history of Hyères is inseparably bound to its saltworks. Salt has always been a popular food preservative, and even the Greeks and Romans reduced seawater into salt in an area east of the city, which was then known as Olbia. Salt production then lay dormant for a long time, but Hyères eventually saw a revival when the Lords of Fos built a fortified town here called Areis, which was protected by a castle complex.

In the era of industrialization, demand for salt once again rose significantly. In response, the Salin des Pesquiers, a 1359-acre saltworks, was established on the narrow strip of land south of Hyères.

The process of salt extraction began with water from the Mediterranean Sea that was passed through several evaporation basins; it was then saturated with chlorine and sodium, thereby increasing the salt content from 3 grams to 260 grams per liter. Every fall, the evaporated sea salt was "harvested" with rakelike tools. The annual yield was close to 40,000 tons. Due to increasing global competition, however, the saltworks of Hyères struggled to operate profitably, and production was finally closed for good in 1995.

In 2001, the salt marshes of the Vieux Salins were taken over by the national coastal protection agency, Le Conservatoire du Littoral, and transformed into an 865-acre nature reserve, which visitors today can explore on designated pathways. There, they gain insights into the reserve's fragile ecosystem from the signage along the trails. Well over 100 different species of birds live in the reserve, including flamingos, cormorants, terns, pied avocets, crested larks, shelducks, herons, and other curlews. In addition, you'll find protected plants such as salicornia, *Limonium* (or sea lavender), and *Suaeda maritima* (or sea blite).

Address Rue de Saint-Nicolas, Village des Vieux Salins, 83400 Hyères, www.tpm-agglo.fr/salins-hyeres | **Getting there** Hyères is located 12.5 miles east of Toulon, at the end of the A 570 highway. The old saltworks stretch another three miles to the east along the coast on the D 12. Best to leave your car at the parking lot marked *Espace Nature*. | **Hours** Jan–Mar, Nov–Dec, Wed–Sun 10am–12pm and 2–4:30pm; Apr–Jun, Sep–Oct, 9am–12pm and 2–5:30pm; July–Aug, 9am–12pm and 4–8pm | **Tip** If you're interested in bird-watching, don't forget your binoculars. It's also worth a quick detour to the Île de Porquerolles south of the peninsula.

29__The Monastery Castle
A fortress of faith

A monastery is a place for retreat and quiet inner contemplation, as its Latin name, *claustrum*, illustrates. Such spots for soul searching were usually built in hard-to-reach locales in remote valleys or on faraway mountain peaks – for the lonelier the location, the fewer worldly influences could disturb the spiritual life of the inhabitants. Therefore, believers often thought of islands as the ideal sites for monasteries – just think of the Mont Saint-Michel in Normandy.

The Île de Saint-Honorat in the Bay of Cannes is considered to be among the first (and therefore oldest) monasteries in Western Europe. It was founded sometime around the year 405 by St. Honoratus, and prospered quickly. In early medieval times, the island was home to hundreds of monks. Thanks to numerous donations, the community occupied an extended property on the mainland as well. But wealth often awakens greed and jealousy: again and again Saracens and other pirates sought out this island home, pillaging and plundering the monastery.

In 1073, the monks finally decided to build a powerful defensive fortress on the southern edge of the island where they could retreat in times of trouble. Their structure resembled a monastery pointing toward the heavens. In order to exercise the monastic life even in the midst of a long siege, the monks converted the courtyard of their fortress into a two-story cloister that included all the usual monastic facilities, such as a refectory, a library, and a chapel. The entrance was 12 feet off the ground and could only be reached using a ladder. Unfortunately, the fortress could not withstand bombardments from the cannons of Spanish and Genoese warships in the 17th century. The island was ultimately conquered, the monastery lost its religious significance, and fell before it was finally abandoned in 1788.

Address 06400 Île de Saint-Honorat | **Getting there** The crossing takes about 15 minutes. Boats depart from Cannes on the western edge of the Vieux Port hourly from 9am; the last crossing is usually at 5:45pm or 6pm. | **Tip** Since 1869, Cistercian monks have once again lived on the island. The old monastery church can be visited (www.abbayedelerins.com).

30_ The Hotel Ruins

The decline of the Hotel Provençal

Juan-les-Pins and the Cap d'Antibes are two of the most prestigious destinations on the French Riviera. Given the area's air of distinguished elegance, it's almost easier to spy Rolls-Royces among the sparse pines here than it is to find yellow taxis in New York City. So if you walk along the coastal road, you might have trouble believing your eyes when you catch sight of the dilapidated colossus towering behind a billboard like a giant white elephant.

The Hotel Provençal is considered the largest hotel ruin in the world, and still bears witness to the heyday of the Côte d'Azur. Thanks to F. Scott Fitzgerald and his wife, Zelda, Antibes and Juan-les-Pins were famous across the Atlantic. The American multimillionaire Frank Jay Gould also enjoyed the area, and in 1927 built this imposing palace with 290 rooms in the trendy Art Deco style of the time. Gould envisioned a luxury hotel that would open for the first time during the summer months, back then still regarded as too hot. His business was a success, and industrialists as well as artists were thrilled. The guests who cavorted in the hotel included Charlie Chaplin, André Gide, Jack Warner, and Estée Lauder.

But the hotel's decline came in 1976: not slowly, but like an earthquake. Its owner at the time, Parisian jeweler Alexandre Reza, decided to close the hotel immediately after his renovation plans were not approved. No one had expected him to actually carry out his threats, but he did, firing all the employees and shuttering the doors. Since then, the hotel has been left to decay. In vain, one looks now for traces of the old splendor through the empty windows of this haunted house. It is crumbling at every corner, and one can only hope that soon an investor will take pity on it and restore it to its former glory.

Address Rue Saint-Barthélémy, 06160 Juan-les-Pins (Antibes) | **Getting there** Juan-les-Pins is located 1.25 miles south of Antibes. The Rue Saint-Barthélémy borders to the east of the Jardins de la Pinède. | **Tip** On the Cap d'Antibes, the Eden Roc, on Boulevard J. F. Kennedy, still affords visitors a luxury hotel that exudes the glamor of bygone days (Tel 0033/(0)493613901, www.hotel-du-cap-eden-roc.com).

31__Jazzy Street Lamps
Swinging lights in New-Orleans-les-Pins

Jazz has been the predominant musical genre in Juan-les-Pins since the Jazz Age in the 1920s, about the same time American writer F. Scott Fitzgerald and his wife, Zelda, gathered together an illustrious group of artists here – to whom the coastal town owes thanks for its giddy flair. At private parties, the best vinyl records were played, including blues, ragtime, spirituals, and jazz, and stars like Maurice Chevalier and Josephine Baker took the stage in clubs.

Even today, neighboring Antibes looks on enviously at the nightlife in Juan-les-Pins. While those in Antibes are turned out onto the sidewalks, the parties rage on in Juan: a half dozen discotheques and at least as many bars are open until the wee hours of the morning. Even the street lighting in town is a throwback to the musical tradition: the colorful, oddly shaped lanterns are reminiscent of the "swinging lights" at the most famous summer jazz festival in Europe, which was founded in 1960.

After World War II, it was the clarinetist and saxophonist Sydney Bechet who had the largest influence on the jazz of the French Riviera. And just a year after his death, the festival was brought to life under the shadow of the eponymous pines. Since then, jazz lovers from all over the world meet each year in July in Juan-les-Pins to listen to the stars of the genre for 10 days under the open sky.

There is probably no known jazz musician who has not already participated in the Jazz-à-Juan Festival in Pinède Gould, including greats such as Ray Charles, Miles Davis, Ella Fitzgerald, and Louis Armstrong, not to mention Oscar Peterson, Dizzy Gillespie, Duke Ellington, Stan Getz, and Keith Jarrett. Numerous musicians – Count Basie, John Coltrane, and Dee Dee Bridgewater – are among those who also immortalized their handprints on the Walk of Fame.

Address Avenue Georges Gallice, 06160 Juan-les-Pins (Antibes) | **Getting there**
Juan-les-Pins is located 1.25 miles south of Antibes. The Avenue Georges Gallice is located
325 feet from the casino. | **Tip** Tickets for the festival are hard to come by, so you should
buy them well in advance (www.jazzajuan.com). In nearby Golf-Juan, a plaque recalls that
in 1815, Napoleon came ashore here after his exile in Elba.

32__ The Dream Pool

The most beautiful pool in the whole Département

"The pool makes the party." This mantra was already old hat to Hollywood stars in the 1930s, who regularly sprawled out in the sun by the pool at the Beverly Hills Hotel. Since those times, there has hardly been a hotel or vacation resort built that does not provide one or more pools in various shapes and sizes for its guests.

There are round, oval, and kidney-shaped basins, the bottoms of which shimmer in various turquoise tones; some have clearly delineated stainless steel tanks or precious mosaic floors with the hotel's initials; others feature fountained terraces and infinity pools, which give the impression that the water has married itself to the horizon. The very sight of a pool promises relaxation, fun, and joie de vivre, and even the smallest pool exudes decadence and luxury, giving off an air of sensuality.

For a long time, swimming pools have also belonged to the cityscape of many French towns, where often they are only open for a couple of months a year. Even tiny La Bollène-Vésubie did not want to be left behind in this trend, although it counts only 500 residents within its borders.

La Bollène-Vésubie is on display for all to see atop a hill in the Maritime Alps. Its view extends far over the chestnut forests and the ridge of peaks of the Mercantour National Park, and then back over to the mighty Massif de l'Authion. A better place for a swimming pool can hardly be imagined.

There was not enough room for an Olympic-sized basin, but the heated pool is at least 25 meters long, so even athletic swimmers have no problem finding room to swim laps. *Matériel de plage* is also available for rent, because the panoramic view over the mountaintops is even more spectacular when seen from a lounge chair under an umbrella.

Address Ancien Chemin de la Bollène, 06020 La Bollène-Vésubie | **Getting there** La Bollène-Vésubie is located 37 miles north of Nice and reached via the M 2565. | **Hours** July–early Sep, daily 11am–7pm | **Tip** Right next to the swimming pool there is also a small restaurant, which is open in the summer.

33___Notre-Dame-des-Fontaines

The Sistine Chapel of the Maritime Alps

The pilgrimage chapel of Notre-Dame-des-Fontaines seems to stand at the end of the world. Toward the close of the 14th century, this simple, single-nave church was built in a secluded valley in the midst of the French Maritime Alps, on the site of a previous building. Only a small spur road leads here, and the church is flanked on the left and right by the French-Italian border range. You can sometimes catch a glimpse of the 7,221-foot-high Mont Saccarel, considered the highest mountain in Liguria, even though its summit lies within French territory.

Hidden among the trees and sitting low in the valley, nobody would suspect that in this simple windowless structure stands the largest fresco cycle in southern France, making it one of the most important historical art attractions of the region. The series is the work of a Piedmontese artist-priest named Giovanni Canavesio, who enjoyed a fine reputation as a traveling painter in the county of Nice during the late 15th century. He worked on the frescoes of the chapel for around 12 years. Since Canavesio painted his murals on dry plaster, strictly speaking these are considered tempera paintings, not actual frescoes.

Canavesio was largely inspired by the apocalyptic books he illustrated in his paintings. The scenes depicted mainly stem from three different revolving themes. In the choir and on the eastern front wall, events from the life of the Virgin Mary are portrayed. He used the side walls for the Passion of the Christ, and the entire western wall he reserved for the Last Judgment. The realistic paintings are fascinating for their intricate details, which are at times rather curious. In one scene for example, Judas hangs from an olive tree with bloody entrails showing, slashed by a demon monkey.

Address 06430 La Brigue | **Getting there** La Brigue lies in a side valley of the Roya, about two miles south of Tende. The chapel can be found 2.5 miles east of La Brigue at the end of a small cul-de-sac (D 43). | **Hours** May–Nov, Mon, Wed–Sun 10am–12:30pm and 2–5:30pm | **Tip** Right below the chapel, the Levense flows past. In the summertime, you can cool your feet in the delightful mountain stream.

34_ Parcours Cyclable

Cycling on an old railway line

France is home to the famous Tour de France, and the enthusiasm for cycling is deeply rooted in its population. Everyone, from bakers to lawyers, shivers with excitement at the sight of a road bike. Especially on weekends, you'll see small groups all over France in their colorful jerseys as they struggle in the draft of their lead cycler over mountain passes and hills. Naturally, the Côte d'Azur is an extremely popular destination for bicyclists. Even former President Nicolas Sarkozy pedals through the countryside, ever smiling, in his sporty outfit.

If you are familiar with the country roads, at times extremely narrow, and the driving habits of the southern French, you know that cycling can be dangerous in these parts. Again and again, there are stories about accidents in the newspapers. Fortunately, at some point locals decided to rehabilitate a disused railway line that had lain broken and dormant for decades.

Newly paved and marked with two lanes, these old train tracks have become the core of a bike trail that will one day extend across the whole of the Département Var, from Six-Fours in the west to Saint-Raphaël at the foot of the red Esterel Mountains. In total, the track will eventually be nearly 75 miles long and pass through 10 municipalities. Currently, about 50 miles have been completed, of which nearly 43 are reserved exclusively for cyclists. Undisturbed by automobile traffic, you can cycle along the coast on the Parcours Cyclable du Littoral, conquering only the smallest of hills and passing through the occasional lighted tunnel.

The coastal rail trail is already considered a great success: the neighboring Département Alpes-Maritimes is now also planning on creating a two-lane bikeway along the entire coast between Menton and Théoule-sur-Mer.

Address 83250 La Londe-les-Maures | **Getting there** La Londe-les-Maures lies along the coastal road (D 98) between Hyères and Le Lavendou. | **Tip** Today there are also numerous posted mountain biking trails on the French Riviera. The annual mountain biking festival Roc d'Azur is held in Fréjus (www.rocazur.com).

35_ Trophée des Alpes

A victory monument for Augustus

For just a moment, let's turn the clock back some 2,000-odd years to a time when the entire Mediterranean was ruled by the Romans. No one could hold back the advances of the Roman legions, and Rome's will was law. But here and there, there were handfuls of people who rebelled against the empire. These groups included the Ligurians, who lived deep in the remote mountain valleys of the Alps, along with other mountain dwellers, and insisted on their independence, repeatedly attacking Roman troops and merchants.

Eventually, the Romans had had enough of the rebellious Alpine peoples. Emperor Augustus sent his stepsons with two legions in the direction of Liguria. And as ordered, Drusus and Tiberius took care of their assignment to the emperor's satisfaction. But the submission of the people was probably only the secondary goal; what was most important was securing the strategic land link between Italy and the province of Gallia Narbonensis.

To commemorate the conquest, the Roman Senate erected a gigantic victory monument in honor of the emperor in the year 7 or 6 BC. A 1,575-foot-high summit pass along the Via Aurelia was chosen for its location, which would later mark the boundary between the Roman Italy and Gaul after Diocletian's reforms of the Empire.

When you see the size of the monument, it is clear that the Ligurians must have been brave adversaries: even from afar, you can make out the 115-foot-tall memorial, badly battered by time. How imposing the Trophée des Alpes must have seemed at first, when it towered nearly 165 feet in the sky! Unfortunately, posterity has not taken good care of the monument: first it was transformed into a castle, and later it even served as a quarry. Only at the beginning of the 20th century was its importance recognized and restoration efforts undertaken.

Address Avenue Albert 1er, 06320 La Turbie | **Getting there** La Turbie is located on the Grande Corniche (D 2564) about three miles above Monaco. | **Hours** Apr–Sep, Tue–Sun 9:30am–1pm and 2:30–6:30pm; Oct–Mar, Tue–Sun 10am–1:30pm and 2:30–5pm | **Tip** At the edge of the park there is a panoramic terrace offering a magnificent view of Monaco and the coast.

36_ Scénoparc Alpha

On the trail of wolves

For centuries, wolves roamed wild through the Maritime Alps, but in 1947 that all came to an end for a time. The *Canis lupus* is considered the natural enemy of farmers and shepherds, and with the help of poison, bullets, and traps, hunters decimated and eventually eliminated the wolf population.

However, in 1992, a pack of wolves wandered back into France from the Italian side of the Alps and soon grew in numbers. Wolves still may not be very popular with those whose livelihood is raising livestock, but they are now protected by law and can only be hunted under certain circumstances.

Despite their increasing population, most hikers rarely encounter a wolf in the wild. But interest in viewing them is high, and so, in 2005, a 25-acre landscaped park (Scénoparc Alpha) was created in the heart of the Mercantour National Park, in order to offer visitors the rare chance to observe an entire pack of wolves in their natural habitat.

Since the park's founding, about two dozen wolves raised in captivity have lived amidst the beautiful mountain scenery at an altitude of almost 5,000 feet in three enclosed areas, each greater than six acres, which can be viewed from special observation points. It's possible, however, that you may have to wait quite a while to catch a glimpse of one of these elusive animals. This isn't a zoo, after all, and the wolves naturally seek cover in the undergrowth of the forest.

The easiest and most spectacular way to experience the wolves is to visit the park during their daily feeding. An information center has also been set up in three former cowsheds. Here visitors can learn – through the aid of videos, diagrams, and multimedia exhibits – about the reintroduction of the species into the region.

Address Chalet d'Accueil du Boréon, Route Départementale 89, 06450 Saint-Martin-Vésubie, www.alpha-loup.com | **Getting there** From Saint Martin-Vésubie, drive about five miles in the direction of Le Boréon on the M 89. | **Hours** Feb–mid-Nov, daily 10am–6pm, last entry at 4:30pm, tours at 11:30am and 2:30pm, feeding at 2:30pm | **Tip** From the end of July until the end of August, there are night tours offered at 8pm (reservations required, Tel 0033/(0)493023369).

37_ The Roundabout

A circular canvas

The French are true lovers of roundabouts. Since the first few cars circled the Arc de Triomphe in Paris in 1907, their enthusiasm has known no bounds. With an unbelievable 30,000 *ronds-points*, France claims ownership of half of the world's existing rotaries.

For a French driver, there seems to be nothing more elegant than to merge into traffic and feel pulled by the magnetic flow of a roundabout, and then subsequently and inconspicuously to leave it once again, happily camouflaged by stubbornly refraining from using any sort of turn signal whatsoever. Especially since 1984, when the controversial right-before-left rule was repealed, French road builders have unconditionally subscribed to the idea of installing rotaries in order to increase traffic flow. It's an understandable endeavor: is there anything worse to a motorist than having to sit at a red light when there are no other cars in sight?

Traffic circles can be found on the French Riviera in all sorts of variations, from one to several lanes and anywhere up to eight exits. Critics are quick to complain about the increased space requirements, but this argument holds little weight in Europe's largest territorial state. And incidentally, a *rond-point* slows down the speed of traffic considerably at its entry point, thereby supposedly increasing safety.

Sometime toward the end of the last century, some resourceful landscape architect or tourism manager (perhaps it was even an imaginative local politician) came up with the idea of using the boring island in the middle of the roundabout as a canvas for advertisements. Since then, there are hardly any that are not decked out with ancient amphorae, wild bulls, or colorful boats. In Le Lavendou, one is decorated with three bronze whale fins in a pool of water, bathed by night in a tranquil blue light.

Address 83980 Le Lavandou | **Getting there** When entering any roundabout, slightly reduce your speed and be ready to brake. If no car is approaching, proceed through the traffic circle at a sensible speed. The roundabout with the three bronze whale fins lies west of town on the coastal road (D 98). | **Tip** If you want, you can also take a second spin around!

38__ The Fish Pond in the Bay

A Roman status symbol

The Roman relics left behind in Fréjus and Nice are widely known, but these aren't the only ones in the region. In numerous smaller coastal towns, archaeologists have repeatedly encountered testimonials to the Roman Empire. In one example, the foundations of Roman villas and baths with precious mosaics were found in Saint-Aygulf and Villepey. In Les Issambres, whose local name is derived from the Roman *Sinus Sambracitanus*, there is also a little-known fishing pool from the Gallo-Roman period.

Nearby, Fréjus was known at the time as *Forum Julii*, and with its 40,000 inhabitants, it was among the largest Roman cities in Gaul. Demand for fresh seafood was therefore quite great and could not always be satisfactorily met by fishermen. During Roman times, having a saltwater pool to stock live fish was considered a status symbol for the elite classes. In Les Issambres, a few underwater walls – relics of an ancient fishing pool, or *vivier gallo-romain* – are still visible in the bay of La Gaillarde; they are the only ones remaining in the whole of France.

The *vivier* in Les Issambres is a cove that's been carved out of the rocks with a length of twenty meters and a width varying from five to twelve meters. The pool once consisted of three basins, all separated by low walls with bronze doors that could be opened and shut to regulate the circulation and flow of water. The vivier provided a natural trap for mullets or congers in the spring during their spawning season. The fish in the pool were then fed with bread and food scraps until they were ready to be eaten.

This *vivier gallo-romain* probably belonged to a Roman villa in the immediate neighborhood. Excavations in the area have also uncovered a mosaic depicting a dolphin swimming between two tridents.

Address Along the coastal road in Les Issambres (83520) | **Getting there** Les Issambres is situated about six miles south of Fréjus along the coastal road (D 559). A sign reading *Vivier gallo-romain* leads to the fishing pool. | **Tip** The small bay is still a popular fishing spot today.

39_ The Dream Castle of Henry Clews

Lifestyles of the rich and eccentric

Born in 1876, Henry Clews Jr. was the son of a rich American stockbroker, but he was much more interested in art than investing. After World War I, he moved with his family to the French Riviera, where he bought the ruins of a castle dating from the 14th century in La Napoule and set about restoring it according to his whims.

The result was a small fairy-tale chateau on the shores of the Mediterranean. Since Henry Clews saw himself as an artist, he took an active role in the restoration work. Clews, who happily ran through the halls in handmade costumes, not only marred the Gothic dining room with peculiar door designs, but created pseudo-medieval ornamental capitals for the outer walls. He also included his own basilica with carved sarcophagi for the masters of the house.

Clews thought of himself as a modern-day Don Quixote and called his servant "Sancho"; he organized tea parties for dogs and once threw a lavish dinner for the "Prince del Drago," where the distinguished guest of honor turned out to be an actual monkey dressed in an evening suit. While his wife, Marie, tended to the gardens, Clews dedicated himself to his portrait busts and often phallic sculptures, in the creation of which he was aided by several masons and an assistant who was responsible for editing and fine modeling.

In 1951, his widow established a foundation that seeks above all to promote young American artists, who often move here for months at a time to live and work. Meanwhile, parts of the castle and the beautiful gardens are accessible to the public. In the summertime, regular art exhibitions, as well as theater and musical performances, are held on-site.

Address Avenue Henry Clews, 06210 Mandelieu-La Napoule, www.chateau-lanapoule.com |
Getting there Mandelieu-La Napoule is about three miles west of Cannes along the
coastal road (D 6098). | **Hours** Daily 10am–6pm except Nov 8–Feb 7, Sat and Sun only
10am–5pm; Mar–Oct, tours at 11:30am, 2:30pm and 4:30pm daily | **Tip** Bring your
swimming gear! There is a sandy beach right in front of the château that is also suitable for
children.

40__ The Stage of War

Ruins that recall battles lost and won

The Massif de l'Authion, which forms a part of the larger Mercantour National Park, is an area that is truly secluded from the world below, both barren and fascinating at the same time. The mountain range extends just above the tree line, at an elevation of more than 6,500 feet, and consistently attracts visitors with its unique flora and fauna. After the snow melts in early summer, plant varieties worthy of protection, such as gentian, edelweiss, and saxifrage, thrive here. With luck, you can also gain special insight into the unique world of the high-altitude fauna: rare bearded vultures and lammergeiers can be seen circling over the peaks, along with chamois, mouflon, and ibex. Visitors are treated to a magnificent panoramic view extending far beyond the southern Alps and Mont Bégo, up to the Alpine peaks that lie beyond the French border and are often blanketed in mysterious mists.

Those who come to explore the Massif de l'Authion quickly realize that it was not always so tranquil. Traces of fortifications, bunkers, rusted tanks, and the ruins of houses are reminders that the mountain range has repeatedly served as a battleground due to its strategically important location.

Early on in the Second Italian War of Independence, in 1793 and 1794, about 30,000 soldiers fought here. Toward the end of World War II, German troops entrenched themselves on the plateau. On April 10, 1945, the French began their attack, which, despite intense resistance, came to a successful conclusion within two weeks. The battle, in which 273 solders were killed and 644 were injured, was among the last acts of war on French territory.

A trip on the circular 5.5-mile-long *Circuit de la Découverte de l'Authion* – which you can take in only one direction – is particularly inspiring.

Address Massif de l'Authion | **Getting there** Right on the Col de Turini, a small winding road branches off to the north (D 68), which leads to the Massif de l'Authion. | **Tip** Since the circular route boasts numerous potholes, it is often more enjoyable to cover the loop with a two or three-hour hike or on a mountain bike.

41_Canyon du Mal Infernet

Dumping ground for the afflicted

Between Cannes and Saint-Raphaël lies the most sparsely populated stretch of the French Riviera. This is due not to the high real-estate prices, but rather to the Massif de l'Estérel, an ancient volcanic mountain range, with its striking red porphyry rocks. Mont Vinaigre, at 2,028 feet, marks its highest point. The landscape has remained largely uninhabited because the meager soil is unsuitable for any cultivation. Most tourists sail past the massif on the coastal road, looking only for somewhere to swim and sunbathe.

Given the sparse vegetation, it is difficult to imagine that a dense cork and holm oak forest once covered the entire mountain range. At that time, the massif served as a retreat and hideout for bandits and highwaymen, who notoriously attacked stagecoaches repeatedly. Their most famous leader was a certain Gaspard de Besse, who was captured in 1781 and executed in Aix-en-Provence. As a deterrent to his comrades, his head was nailed to a tree that stood directly on the main route through the Estérel Mountains.

Due to numerous forest fires, today the massif is mainly overgrown with dense and wild bushy shrubs known in the Mediterranean as *maquis*.

From Col de Belle Barbe, one can easily hike along the Grenouillet River in the direction of Lac l'Ecureuil. However, this reservoir has been largely dried up for several years. On the hour-and-a-half hike, you'll pass through the surprisingly green Canyon du Mal Infernet, whose name recalls the fact that people who were suffering from the plague in the Middle Ages were often thrown into the ravine. You can continue from the reservoir up to the Pic de l'Ours for an hour-long hike on the red-and-white marked trail. The 1614-foot-high peak is crowned with striking signal masts and is therefore hard to miss.

Address Massif de l'Estérel, above 83530 Agay | **Getting there** Reached via the D 100.
Those coming from Agay will reach a small sign reading *Massif de l'Estérel* after about three
miles. Follow this road for about a mile and a quarter, and you'll find a small parking lot at
the foot of the Col de Belle Barbe on the left-hand side. | **Tip** There are no places to buy
food or drinks, so be sure to bring provisions with you. In Agay, there is a great bay for
swimming.

42___ The Bastion of Art

How Jean Cocteau beautified the city

Jean Cocteau had a special relationship with Menton. As far back as 1957, he was invited by then mayor Francis Palmero to redesign the wedding hall in the municipal building in any way he wanted. The painter-poet did not hesitate long and created an alternative to the bare and dreary atmosphere typically found in most French registry offices. As his motif, Cocteau chose an allegorical wedding scene with allusions to Orpheus and Eurydice, the front wall dominated by a young couple with eyes only for each other. And of course, above the entire scene, the artist rides atop a Pegasus.

Cocteau's wedding hall proved to be a clever marketing move on the mayor's part to pep up the image of the conservative city previously known only for its lemons – to this day it is one of the most popular attractions in Menton. The *Salle des Mariages* is a fascinating work of art; in France there is hardly a more beautiful setting for a wedding, since Cocteau curated everything from the lighting and furniture down to the mirrors in the entryway. French couples aren't the only ones lining up to exchange their vows here, approximately 20 couples a year travel all the way from Japan to be married before the unique backdrop.

While painting the hall, Jean Cocteau took numerous walks through Menton (he praised the houses of the old city as "exquisite small fortresses in pastel colors, the appearance of their asymmetrical facades reminds me of a human face"), where he discovered a port bastion standing empty. The city of Menton was happy to let him redesign it, too, according to his fancy. With specially designed wall mosaics, ceramics, drawings, and tapestries, Cocteau transformed the bastion into a very personal museum, where his aura can still be felt today. *"Je reste avec vous"* is written under a relief bearing his likeness.

Address Quai Napoléon III, 06500 Menton | **Getting there** Located on the harbor bastion. | **Hours** Oct–Apr, Mon, Wed–Sun 10am–12pm and 2–6pm, May–Sep, until 7pm | **Tip** In the fall of 2011, another Cocteau museum opened in Menton, with the futuristic Musée Jean Cocteau (Collection Séverin Wunderman). More than 1,500 objects are on display (Sep–June, Mon, Wed–Sun 10am–6pm, July and Aug, 10am–10pm, www.museecocteaumenton.fr).

43__ The Flight of Steps
A cinematic setting

Menton shows its best side to those who view it from the harbor or beach. Its pastel-colored houses climb up the hillside, and the entire scene is crowned by the mighty Basilica of Saint-Michel. The home fronts along the Quai Bonaparte seal off the old town, pierced in only one place by a monumental staircase. This beautiful flight of stairs paved with pebbles was built to compensate for the difference in height between the Plage des Sablettes and the church square. A ramplike structure leads up to the Parvis de St-Michel.

These steps have served several times as a backdrop for fashion shoots and film productions, such as the James Bond movie *Never Say Never Again*, easily recognizable when Sean Connery races past the basilica on a motorcycle during a car chase. And in *Grace of Monaco*, Oscar-winner Nicole Kidman climbs the stairs sporting a stylish headscarf and sunglasses.

Arriving at the top, you will find yourself on the square in front of the Basilica of Saint-Michel. An oversized mosaic depicting the coat of arms of the Grimaldi family adorns the square, which resembles an Italian piazza and reminds us that Menton – as well as neighboring Roquebrune – was for centuries a part of the Principality of Monaco.

From the plaza in front of the church there is a magnificent view of the coast and across the border into Italy. The ocher-colored cathedral is a powerful three-aisled Baroque construction, in whose form and design you will notice distinctly Italian influences. The interior, decorated with stucco and frescoes, fits into the zeitgeist with its perspective paintings. From the building dating from the Middle Ages that previously stood on this spot, only the smaller of the two bell towers can still be seen; the larger is divided into floors like an Italian campanile.

Address Quai Bonaparte, 06500 Menton | **Getting there** Located at the eastern edge of the old city. | **Tip** The International Chamber Music Festival (Festival de Musique), with its moving evening concerts, is held during the first half of August in front of the Église Saint-Michel (www.musique-menton.fr).

44__Jardin Fontana Rosa
The garden of the poets

Shielded from the cold and wind by the foothills of the Maritime Alps, no other city along the French and Italian Riviera is more spoiled by a lovely climate than Menton. Thanks to this natural protection, countless species of exotic plants thrive in roughly two dozen botanical gardens throughout the city.

Most of these gardens, along with numerous impressive villas dating from the Belle Epoque period, can be found in the suburb of Garavan, including the Jardin de la Villa Marina Serena and the Jardin Exotique du Val Rahmeh, overgrown with tropical plants.

The Jardin Fontana Rosa certainly counts among the most unusual in the neighborhood. It is not only a garden, but, to a certain extent, a poetic bequest. When the Spanish writer Vicente Blasco Ibañez (1867 – 1928) fled the Spanish military dictatorship and found himself in Menton, he had a magnificent villa built, surrounded by grounds designed in the Andalusian-Arab style. Unfortunately, the villa had to be torn down in 1985 due to disrepair, but the garden was preserved and, luckily for us, still looks much like it used to. In 1990 it was declared an historic monument.

The colorful entrance gate shines with ceramic portraits of Charles Dickens, Honoré de Balzac, and Miguel de Cervantes. In the garden, laid out like a reading room, a unique world opens up before you. It almost appears Ibañez created it in order to pay homage to his favorite authors. Cervantes, considered a saint in his home country of Spain, even has a semicircular temple-like area dedicated to him.

Those who wander among the benches, columns, pergolas, and fountains, all decorated with ceramics, will discover references to the writers revered by Ibañez and immortalized in the garden, including Zola, Flaubert, Hugo, Tolstoy, Dostoyevsky, and Poe.

Address Avenue Blasco Ibañez, 06500 Menton | **Getting there** A half mile east of the old city, turn north from the Porte de France. | **Hours** Guided tours Mon and Fri at 10am | **Tip** The Parc du Pian is the only park in Menton that is populated by the olive tree, the typical vegetation of the Mediterranean region. In the summer, concerts are often held here.

45 Jardin Serre de la Madone

An English garden of dreams

The Englishman Sir Lawrence Johnston (1871–1958) was an enthusiastic garden lover. Johnston's Hidcote Manor Garden, located in the county of Hertfordshire, is considered to be one of the most beautiful English gardens of the 20th century, with its artfully trimmed plants and perennial beds. After its installation was largely completed, Johnston acquired a hillside plot of land in Gorbiotal in 1924, in the town of Menton. Johnston took advantage of the area's unique microclimate and built a garden called the Jardin Serre de la Madone.

The site, which had previously been used to grow wine grapes and olives, was transformed by Johnston, with each of its 22 terraces conceived of as a unique planting space. A wide stone staircase leads up to a Victorian villa. You can wander through the site, which covers an area of more than 17 acres, under shady trees and pergolas, among which grow exotic flora such as trumpet flowers and fig trees, although their fruit is not suitable for consumption. Each season, the garden is immersed anew in a wash of colors. Fountains, statues, and ornately decorated stone benches serve as focal points and offer spots from which to take in the scenery. A water garden framed by cypresses and pine trees is the central element: a dreamlike scenario with blooming water lilies, a statue of Mary mirrored in the water of the fountain, and a greenhouse for orange trees.

After Johnston's death, the garden began to fall into disrepair, but in 1990 the city of Menton succeeded in naming La Serre de la Madone as the first garden site in France under memorial protection, thereby keeping at bay real-estate speculators looking to make a land grab. The garden was finally acquired in 1999 by the Conservatoire du Littoral, and has now been carefully restored.

Address 74 Route de Gorbio, 06500 Menton, www.serredelamadone.com | **Getting there** Northwest of the city, along the road to Gorbio (D 23). | **Hours** Apr–Oct, Tue–Sun 10am–6pm, Dec–Mar, 10am–5pm; Nov closed. Those who speak French should definitely take one of the garden tours, held at 3pm. | **Tip** The Musée des Beaux-Arts du Palais Carnolès, located at 3 Avenue de la Madone, displays classical paintings (Oct–Mar, Wed–Mon 10am–12pm and 2–6pm, Apr–Sep, 10am–1pm and 2–6pm).

46_ The Tourist Cemetery

Passing through and away in Menton

In the 19th century, just as in the rest of the French Riviera, Menton was considered an ideal place to spend the winter due to its mild climate, which was helpful for overcoming illnesses. The Swiss cultural historian Jacob Burckhardt remarked smugly in 1881 regarding these *hivernants*: "As far as the Riviera is concerned, if the current times of luxury were to continue in the same manner, in a few years it will be nothing more than a single hotel, where all the rich and sick of Europe spend their winter. In those moments when the sea is calm, you'll hear nothing more than a cough."

The sanatorium was home to a morbid community, where the numbers thinned out progressively as the winter dragged on, because for many guests the high humidity in the sunny south had fatal health consequences. In the cemeteries of Nice, Menton, and Cannes, you can still see many names of Russian nobles and British officers. To quote Guy de Maupassant: "How truly in every part of the world, this lovely and terrible spot must be accursed, this anteroom of Death, perfumed and sweet …"

In 1807, the Cimetière du Vieux Château in Menton was built around the ruins of an old castle, an impressive symbol of that epoch, as it was where numerous northern Europeans found their final resting place. The magnificent tombstones are distributed over four terraces – one for each denomination – and includes the graves of Polish princes such as Pierre Traobetzkoy, German nobles such as Hermann von Ludendorff, and the Reverend William Webb Ellis, who is considered the inventor of rugby. It is truly one dignified resting place: even Gustave Flaubert found the unique location and the aura of the cemetery appealing, with its prominent position overlooking the city and the sea, the view extending over the old harbor and the bay of Garavan.

Address Rue du Vieux Château, 06500 Menton | **Getting there** The Cimetière du Vieux Château is situated above the village on the Montée du Souvenir. | **Hours** Daily 7am–8pm, in the winter months until 6pm | **Tip** The narrow Rue Longue, which leads from the old city to the cemetery, is one of the most romantic streets in Menton.

47_Église Sainte-Dévote

Where a fishing boat ran aground

Day after day, crowds of tourists pour into Monaco. Bus by bus, cruise ship by cruise ship, the principality is overrun. The flow goes up into the old city from the prince's palace, to the oceanic museum, on to the Cathédrale Notre-Dame, and then into the casino and to the exotic garden.

Nobody pays any attention to the small church dedicated to Sainte-Dévote, however, because it stands apart from the main tourist attractions in the Vallon des Gaumates, and hardly any visitor knows that the relics of the patron saint of Monaco are housed within its walls. Even the popular cultural and artistic guides to Monaco don't mention the saint or the church. Sainte-Dévote is in itself an insider's tip.

Dévote became a Christian legend on the basis of her faith, which she would not renounce, and she was therefore tortured to death in Corsica. The Christians took possession of her body in order to bring it to Africa, but during the voyage they were overtaken by a storm. Then from Dévote's mouth rose a dove, which the fishing boat followed until finally it ran aground on the coast of Monaco. (A quick heretical question: Has anyone ever actually counted the number of saints that happen to get stranded somewhere along the coast of the Mediterranean? There must be dozens, if not hundreds.) Well, just at the point where said fishing boat ran aground, a small chapel was erected, which was, over the years, rebuilt several times. Today's church dates only from 1870.

Monaco is, incidentally – gambling notwithstanding – a deeply religious place, so Sainte-Dévote is still revered today as the patron saint of the small country. It is traditional for the bride of the prince of Monaco to lay her bouquet in the church of Sainte-Devote after the couple's wedding ceremony – just as Grace Kelly did in 1956.

Address Place Sainte-Dévote, 98000 Monaco, www.diocese.mc | **Getting there** Located on the coastal road at the northern end of Port Hercule. | **Hours** Daily 8am–6pm | **Tip** In the early evening of January 26, the faithful gather at the harbor *quai*, where a boat is burned, and the relics of Saint Dévote are escorted to the church in a solemn procession.

48_ The Escalator

Monaco's unusual means of transport

Those who think that the Principality of Monaco is a feudal city-state dominated by decrepit ancient structures are sorely mistaken. The principality is in constant motion: it goes up and down, over and under, high and low. Now, we're not talking about stock prices or housing costs (those only go up), instead we're referring to the elevators and escalators, without which you won't get far in Monaco.

A permanent lack of space prevails in the tiny state, and with about 18,000 residents per square kilometer, Monaco boasts the highest population density in the world. There is such a dearth of land that the train station had to be built underground. The tiny principality is exactly two square kilometers, and because it lies at the foot of the Maritime Alps, its high-rise buildings must climb up a steep slope from the sea. To overcome the height differences, which at times can be quite considerable, there are many public elevators and escalators. They represent an important link between the individual parts of the city, but visitors are often hopelessly confused with their staggered and unclear course. Fortunately, there is also a good bus system, but you really can't get by without the elevators and escalators.

The escalators are more user-friendly and offer you the advantage of being able to see your destination up ahead, but the elevators are a true mystery to foreigners. Again and again, secret entrances open up, magically sucking in or spitting out passengers. The cryptic labels are comprehensible only to the initiated. There are even elevators that must inform their passengers: *Laissez le doigt appuyé pendant la durée de la course* ("Hold the button down the entire way until you have reached your destination"). Fortunately, the doors open just before your finger starts to cramp up.

Address Place du Canton, 98000 Monaco | **Getting there** Located directly beneath the Rock of Monaco at the Jardin Animalier. | **Tip** A great view is also available on a trip aboard the solar-powered Bateau Bus, which shuttles people to and from the port daily from 8am to 8pm.

49_ Stade Louis II

Hidden soccer happiness

Those familiar with the legendary soccer stadiums of the world, such as Old Trafford in Manchester or the Stade de France in Paris, will wonder where in the principality the stadium of the soccer club AS Monaco is hidden. According to its website, it is located in Fontvieille, the artificially created part of the city that was wrested with great difficulty from the sea a few decades ago in order to enlarge the territory of Monaco by a bit less than 75 acres.

As you trudge through the streets below the old city, you'll come upon a modern residential area and shopping center, but the Stade Louis II is still nowhere in sight. You might start to wonder if perhaps the stadium was built underground, like the train station, when you suddenly come face-to-face with a downright boring concrete facade, which looks more like a multiplex cinema or parking garage than a monumental stadium. The latter assumption is not totally off base, since the stadium, with its 18,523 seats (standing room would be as out of place in Monaco as a group of rowdy soccer hooligans), was built directly on top of a four-story car park.

Since 1985, AS Monaco has played its home matches in the Stade Louis II. Since there is, understandably, no national football (soccer) league in Monaco, the team takes part in French league play. It is a member of the French Football Federation and has achieved an impressive list of accomplishments: AS Monaco has been French soccer champions and cup winners several times and has competed in numerous international contests. Stars like David Trezeguet, Thierry Henry, Fabien Barthez, and Jürgen Klinsmann have played on the teams of Monaco's clubs. After a two-year interlude in the second division starting in 2013, AS Monaco hopes to soon return to its former glory.

Address 7 Avenue des Castelans, 98000 Monaco | **Getting there** The stadium is located west of the Rock of Monaco. | **Hours** French and English tours Mon–Fri at 10:30am, 11:30am, 2:30pm, 4pm, and 5pm | **Tip** Purchase game tickets from the club's website (www.asm-fc.com) or – since the stadium is rarely sold out – from the box office on game days.

50__Notre Dame de la Menour

The great wall of France

Every year in January, things get lively in the hinterland of the French Riviera. During the legendary Rallye Monte Carlo road race, the snowy mountain lanes pose a real challenge for drivers. The most famous stage of the race, the "night of the long knives," is full of tight hairpin curves up to the Col de Turini, at a height of 5,272 feet. It is often this leg that decides the ultimate winners.

Although the speed is relatively low here because of the numerous turns, drivers must be careful not to avert their gaze even for a second toward the Chapelle Notre Dame de la Menour, which sits on the side of the road. It's a real shame, too, because the chapel, with its yellow Renaissance facade, is surely among the most beautifully situated churches in the Maritime Alps. A picturesque bridge supported by several arches stretches across the road, its moss covered steps leading visitors up to the chapel, perched atop a small conical mountain peak. The building is actually Romanesque, but was given a more "modern" facade in the 16th century.

The idyllic scenery and long bridge – itself reminiscent of a section of the Great Wall of China – carry visitors away to another world. Few tourists ever visit the church, and it is a sublime experience to cross the lonely road. Unfortunately, the chapel is almost always closed, but the view over the ravines of the Piaon River and its forests, known for their porcini mushrooms, is quite impressive. If possible, visit in the evening, when the facade is illuminated in the mild light of the setting sun. The stillness of the place is only interrupted three times a year: on Easter, Pentecost, and on the 8th of September, when the residents of the nearby village of Moulinet make a pilgrimage up the mountain for a mass in the chapel, and the bridge and square burst into life.

Address 06086 Moulinet | **Getting there** About six miles north of Sospel, the church stands along the D 2566, which leads to Moulinet. There is a small parking lot along the road. | **Tip** Moulinet has a nice shady village square, where you can find the restaurant Le Grain de Sel. The specialty of the house is the cassolette with porcini mushroom ravioli (www.resto-graindesel.fr).

51__Chez Palmyre
Cooking traditions à la niçoise

The old city is the nerve center of Nice. And in the maze of its streets, which occupy the small triangle between Castle Hill, the waterfront promenade, and the parks of the Paillon River, the smell of freshly baked *socca* wafts through the air. At numerous stalls, patties as big as wagon wheels are cooked, made mainly of chickpea flour. This fast food *à la niçoise* is a belly filler, and as cheap as it is tasty.

But there are also several restaurants in the old city that know how to prepare an authentic and traditional home-cooked meal. A classic favorite is the Chez Palmyre. This neighborhood institution, which was opened in 1926 by Palmyre Moni, still satisfies its guests with its simple living-room atmosphere, dominating counter, and exposed brick walls. Originally the restaurant was a typical family affair, and the day-to-day offerings comprised a small selection of market-fresh dishes at reasonable prices. Palmyre and her daughter Suzanne took all the orders and puttered around in the small kitchen, separated from the dining room only by a curtain. Her husband sat enthroned behind the counter like a patron, getting up every now and again to answer the phone, but otherwise staying put (so as not to worry anyone that he was overexerting himself).

In 2010, Suzanne had to give up the family enterprise due to her age, but the new owners, Vincent Verneveaux (chef) and Philippe Terranova (service manager), have not only continued running Chez Palmyre in the same traditional manner, they have found subtle ways to refine and improve the concept. Solid home cooking is still served, which is basic but not without sophistication. Whether you choose the cod puree, the sardine rillettes with eggplant caviar, or a warm potato salad with duck confit, you will not be disappointed.

Address 5 Rue Droite, 06000 Nice, Tel 0033/(0)493857232 | **Public transit** Tramway Cathédrale Vieille Ville | **Hours** Mon–Fri open for lunch and dinner, reservations recommended | **Tip** The Acchiardo at 38 Rue Droite is another unpretentious restaurant in the old town (Mon–Fri; closed for vacation in Aug, Tel 0033/(0)493855116).

52__Climatisation Naturelle
Old school AC

Summers on the French Riviera are hot, and on some days a sweltering heat hangs heavy over Nice and makes living an all but paralyzing activity. Above all, the roofs and the upper floors of homes and buildings heat up to such an extent that they are almost uninhabitable. Those that have air-conditioning are definitely fortunate.

But a few centuries ago you could not just flip a switch to turn on the AC as you can today, and the builders of the past had to be creative and solve the problem using their heads – as well as physics and the laws of temperature exchange. As you walk through the streets of the old city today, you can still observe many of the so-called *clairoirs*. These are rounded openings, placed directly over the front door of a house. Sometimes they are integrated into stone portals, other times they are cut right through the walls, and a number are fitted with wrought-iron bars.

These *clairoirs* are not only a design element – they are also referred to as *climatisation naturelle* (natural climate control) because they work like oversized chimneys. Since the narrow streets of the old town lie mostly in the shade, they are cooler than the upper floors of the surrounding houses. This difference in temperature is enough to set the air in motion, so that the laundry hung in the streets dries very quickly. Together with other architectonic elements, such as the shutters typically found in Nice, which have flaps that lie slightly open to the street, the *clairoirs* use the natural flow of air so that cold air is drawn in and flows through the hallways and the narrow courtyard and then up into the stairwell, cooling the building in the process. On the roof, the air then escapes through a special hatch. You can still observe about 60 of these cooling vents today in the old city.

Address 06000 Nice | **Public transit** Tramway Cathédrale Vieille Ville | **Tip** The oldest of the *clairoirs*, located at 13 Rue de la Condamine, dates from 1485.

53_ The Ice-Cream Parlor
Well worth the wait

Fenocchio is no simple ice-cream parlor, because Francis Fenocchio is a *Maitre Glacier* (as is written with pride on the awning and the storefront). The long lines that form in the summer in front of the shop are further testament to the popularity of the ice cream sold in a white cup with *Fenocchio* written across it in pink lettering.

The art of making ice cream is known to have originated in Italy. What luck, then, that Nice was a part of the Italian state until 1860, and that today there are several wonderful ice-cream parlors in the city on the Bay of Angels. The Fenocchio family enterprise, however, is the most famous and best ice-cream shop in Nice.

Since 1966, Fenocchio has sold his confections in the old city, where his reputation was built on the great variety and unusual flavors he offers. There is a selection of nearly 100 ice creams to choose from, including olive, lavender, ginger, and avocado. For those looking to quench their thirst with a cold brew, the menu even features a scoop of beer-flavored ice cream, which the proprietors guarantee will not make you drunk. But if you're not feeling this adventurous, no worries: classic flavors like vanilla, chocolate, and pistachio are always available. Today, the ice cream is no longer produced on-site, but in its own small factory in the suburb of La Gaude, using only high-quality ingredients that come mostly from local suppliers.

The shop offers not just ice cream, but also around 35 varieties of sorbet, including rosemary and tomato and basil, as well as fruity options such as purple fig.

There are also around a dozen styles of ice-cream cakes, such as delicate creations like the *Comté de Nice*, made with pine nuts and candied mandarin oranges, which harks back to the old culinary traditions of the city.

Address 2 Place Rossetti, 06300 Nice. www.fenocchio.fr | **Public transit** Tramway Cathédrale Vieille Ville | **Hours** Mar–Nov, daily 9am–midnight, closed Dec–Feb | **Tip** There is also a branch in the old town at 6 Rue de la Poissonerie.

54_ Gare du Sud

The nearly demolished station of the Train des Pignes

"Mirror, mirror on the wall, who's the fairest train station of them all?" Nice's central station could certainly make a valid claim for the honor. After all, it is the oldest and most important train station in the city. The powerful, wide facade of the building with its central pavilion is an imposing example of station architecture of the 19th century. But alas, there is another contender in this beauty pageant.

A few hundred yards north stands a second charming railway-station building, which almost fell victim to the wrecking ball. The Gare du Sud, built in 1892, was designed by architect Prosper Bobin in the neoclassical style and dates from a period in which there were several competing railway companies in the region. While the main railway station served the line from Marseille to Italy, the Chemin de Fer du Sud de la France was another company that maintained more local lines, to Dignes-les-Bains, for example. These narrow-gauge railways ran mostly through very mountainous terrain, and the trains designed to use them were not compatible with other lines.

After World War II, the local-line railway company ran into financial difficulties, and all lines were shut down with the exception of the famous Train des Pignes, which runs through the Maritime Alps as far as Digne-les-Bains. The imposing railway station with its terminal building and its rear metal extension slowly fell into disrepair and was replaced in 1991 by a small alternative station, which could easily claim the title of "ugliest train station in Nice." Thanks to numerous public protests, plans to demolish the beautiful Gare du Sud were taken off the table and the city decided instead to renovate the building. Since December 2013, the Gare du Sud has sparkled with newfound luster, and now is home to a multi-media resource center.

Address Avenue Malausséna, 06000 Nice | **Public transit** Tramway Libération | **Tip** It is worth taking a ride on the Train des Pignes, also known as the pinecone train, to Digne-les-Bains. The nearly 100-mile route takes about three hours (www.trainprovence.com).

55_ The Garibaldi Monument

Italy: so close and yet so far

Nice is the city of Giuseppe Garibaldi. The famous freedom fighter – who more than any other single person deserves credit for the unification of Italy – was born in the city on July 4, 1807, the son of a ship captain. Italian was spoken in Nice at that time, because the city was for centuries a part of the Italian states of Savoy or Piedmont. This rich Italian history is still reflected today in the houses and facades of the old city.

Garibaldi loved his hometown wholeheartedly, and he extolled it as "one of the most beautiful areas in this my unfortunate and yet radiant fatherland"; but he loved Italy even more, and he longed for its unity. Garibaldi took part in multiple uprisings and revolutions, and as a result had to spend many years in exile outside of Europe. His goal was the national unity of the many countries splintered into various principalities and kingdoms. In 1860, he landed in Marsala with his legendary "redshirts," and paved the way for the unification of the Italian national state through the conquest of Sicily. In an ironic twist of fate, however, the price for the realization of Garibaldi's dream of unification was that the Italian Kingdom of Sardinia had to cede the county of Nice to France. The newly unified Italian government that came together in 1861 "thanked" the French for their support in the struggle against Austria with the cession of Nice, although in the trade they extended their own territory to include Lombardy.

In Nice, Giuseppe Garibaldi has never been forgotten: while he was still alive, a plaza on the edge of the old city was named for him, and since 1891, a monument has stood in his honor. The work, created by the sculptors Antoine Étex and Gustave Deloye, depicts the freedom fighter in his "redshirt," his gaze, naturally, turned in the direction of Turin.

Address Place Garibaldi, 06000 Nice | **Public transit** Tramway Garibaldi | **Tip** Right under the arcades of the Place Garibaldi, at number 5, is the Grand Café de Turin, which opened in 1908 and is the quintessential place to eat fresh seafood in Nice. A plate crowded with crabs, oysters, sea urchins, and various mussels is served on ice, and looks like a still life (Tel 0033/(0)493622952, www.cafedeturin.com).

56 Hotel Excelsior
The former Gestapo headquarters

Modern and freshly renovated, the Hotel Excelsior is situated in a pretty Belle Epoque building from the 19th century. Subtle colors, a beautiful wood floor, and a comprehensive wellness concept ensure that guests of the four-star hotel feel right at home. On the hotel website, Nice is presented as a holiday metropolis with historical elegance, but there is no mention of the history and previous use of the building itself. This is understandable, on the one hand, because it is a sensitive issue, and who wants to advertise that guests can spend their holiday in a former Gestapo headquarters? On the other hand, the Excelsior was a hotel long before it was abused by the Nazis for almost 360 days. How did this come to pass?

After their allies, the Italians, signed an armistice and subsequently exited the theater of the war, German troops and the Gestapo marched over the Var and invaded Nice. Several luxury hotels, including L'Hermitage in Cimiez, served as military headquarters, while the Gestapo, under the command of the infamous SS Captain Alois Brunner, resided in the Hotel Excelsior.

Night after night, Nazi henchmen fanned out across the city. The suspects they rounded up were interrogated and tortured at the hotel. The Excelsior was considered the forecourt to deportation. During the period prior to August 28, 1944, more than 3,000 Jews, including 264 children, were deported from Nice and the surrounding area, first to Drancy and then to the concentration camps. Arno Klarsfeld was counted among those victims. For the father of French lawyer Serge Klarsfeld – the man who would later be known as the Nazi hunter – thus began an ordeal that ended with his murder in Auschwitz.

A memorial plaque was unveiled outside the Excelsior on October 9, 2009.

Address 19 Avenue Durante, 06000 Nice, www.excelsiornice.com | **Public transit** Tramway Gare Thiers | **Tip** There are several memorial plaques in Nice that remember the Resistance fighters and Jews; at the train station a plaque memorializes the deportation of Jews.

57__ The House of the Exiled Writers

A home away from home

Nice, along with Marseille and Sanary-sur-Mer, was one of those cities in the South of France where many well-known writers and intellectuals found themselves in exile after the Nazis seized power in Germany.

Among the politically uprooted were the three authors and friends: Hermann Kesten, Joseph Roth, and Heinrich Mann. Together, they rented a house in the fall of 1934 with three furnished apartments on the Promenade des Anglais (house number 121, on the corner of the Petite Avenue de la Californie).

On the first floor, Hermann Kesten lived with his wife, Toni; while on the second floor, Joseph Roth lived with "the beautiful" Manga Bell, and the third floor housed Heinrich Mann and his second wife, Nelly Kroeger. In his memoir, *My Friends, the Poets*, Hermann Kesten described this as a rather carefree time, despite their exile: "On blue evenings we stood on our balconies and watched as the sun set into the sea. Its reflection reddened the waves and the sky and the cheeks of our ladies. Sunnily we spent the following months here together."

They began their mornings by diligently working on their texts, and met later in the day at the Café de France or under the arcades of the Place Masséna at the Café Monnod to discuss the "laws of the historical novel." At the time, all three of the authors had submerged themselves in research for novels whose action played out in the past: Heinrich Mann wrote *Henri Quarte*; Hermann Kesten, *Ferdinand and Isabella*; and Joseph Roth, *The Hundred Days* (about Napoleon's return from Elba). In so doing, the trio could at least temporarily banish the political present from their own works.

Address 121 Promenade des Anglais, 06200 Nice | **Public transit** Bus lines 3, 5, and 7 | **Tip** Magnus Hirschfeld died on May 14, 1935, from a stroke. His grave can be found in the Cimetière de Caucadis. His motto has been engraved on his tombstone: "*Per scientiam ad iustitiam*" (Justice through science).

58__Maison Bestagno
Umbrella heaven

While meandering through the streets of the old city and happening upon a small, ancient corner store offering customers umbrellas of all shapes and sizes, you'd be forgiven for thinking Nice must have terrible weather. But wait, a shop for umbrellas in a city that is known to have 280 days of sunshine per year? Is that really necessary?

The answer is a resounding, "Yes!" The Maison Bestagno was opened in 1850 by the great-great-great uncle of the shop's current owner. Since then, umbrellas (*parapluies*), parasols (*ombrelles*), and walking sticks (*cannes*) have been sold in the store with the pretty wooden facade. The selection inside is huge: there are mini umbrellas, telescoping umbrellas, and umbrellas that are large enough to comfortably spend a romantic afternoon underneath on the pebbly beach even in a heavy rain. There are monochromatic ones and colorful ones, those with polka dots and those in plaid. Fashionable eccentrics will enjoy the handmade umbrellas with impressionist motifs and real wood handles, including, naturally, a model with a printed image of Renoir's famous painting *The Umbrellas*.

The small parasols are also fanciful, made out of soft fabrics and edged with fringe if you so desire. A large portion of the umbrellas are produced on-site and manufactured on the second floor of the building, where repairs are also made. In all of France, there are only two other shops that exclusively sell umbrellas still in existence.

The walking sticks are a special hobby of Monsieur Gino Bestagno. He has a whole collection of historical canes, which – whether curved, made of silver, or adorned with ivory – were once an integral part of the fashionable outfits of noble gentlemen, but unfortunately have now disappeared completely from the Promenade des Anglais.

Address 17 Rue de la Préfecture, 06300 Nice, www.maisonbestagno.fr | **Public transit** Tramway Cathédrale Vieille Ville | **Hours** Tue–Sat 9:30am–12pm and 2:30–7pm, closed for vacation in Aug; when it's raining, the shop is also open on Mondays. | **Tip** There are delicious treats to be devoured in the long-standing pastry shop – since 1820! – at 7 Rue Saint-François de Paule (Mon–Sat, Tel 0033/(0)493857798, www.maison-auer.com).

59__ The Matisse House
As colorful as a painter's palette

The Cours Saleya, where Nice's famous flower market is held each day, is one of the most popular squares in the city. Day in and day out, thousands of visitors stroll through the market, and in the evenings the cafés are filled with both tourists and locals. There is no memorial plaque and no sign, however, to point out that Henri Matisse once lived in the house on the eastern edge of the plaza.

When Matisse arrived in Nice in December 1917, he did not care much for the gloomy and rainy city. He lived for a while at the Hôtel Beau-Rivage on the Promenade des Anglais and was preparing to leave when suddenly the Mistral wind swept the clouds from the sky and caused him to rethink his departure.

Matisse was so inspired by the light and play of colors that he decided to stay and sketch the French Riviera. From 1921 to 1938, he lived and worked on the Cours Saleya, in the pretty ocher-yellow building whose facade was so wonderfully lit by the afternoon sun. For the first five years, he lived in an apartment on the third floor overlooking the flower market, then he rented two apartments on the fourth floor, wrapped by balconies, with stunning views of the sea that provided constant inspiration. Matisse decorated his studio with fabrics, carpets, and curtains, and it was here that he created *Odalisque with Raised Arms* and other important works.

Just like Renoir and Picasso, Matisse, too, spent his later years on the Riviera. Toward the end of World War II, he fled for a time to Venice, where he left behind an impressive altarpiece as a decoration in the Chapelle Notre-Dame du Rosaire. During the final few years before his death, Matisse lived in an apartment in the former Hotel Regina Palace in the Cimiez neighborhood of Nice. He died on November 3, 1954, and was buried in the cemetery of Cimiez.

Address Cours Saleya, official address: 1 Place Charles-Félix, 06300 Nice | **Public transit** Tramway Cathédrale Vieille Ville | **Tip** Don't miss a visit to the Musée Matisse, in which numerous paintings from throughout the artist's career are displayed. The museum is located in the Cimiez neighborhood, at 164 Avenue des Arènes de Cimiez (bus lines 15, 17, 20, and 22). Open daily except Tuesday from 10am to 6pm (www.musee-matisse-nice.org).

60___ The Post Office

A postal palace in red brick

In 1990, the former authority responsible for mail, telegraphs, and telephones (PTT) was dismantled and split up. *La Poste* today is dedicated only to letter and parcel delivery, but is still the largest employer in the country after the civil service. A hundred years ago, however, the PTT was the center of national communication and a powerful organization in France.

In 1930, a new central post office was constructed for the growing city on a corner lot very close to the main railway station. The Poste Theirs, with its red brick construction and striking, 27-meter-high clock tower, is the only brick building in the entire city, with 300,000 bricks allegedly used in its construction. The design came from Guillaume Tronchet, a fact held fast in an inscription on the building's northwest tower. Because Tronchet as chief architect was responsible for "civic buildings and national palaces" in all of France, there arose a persistent rumor that the post office was originally designed for the city of Lille in the north of France, where a brick building would have fit much more appropriately into the cityscape. Contemporaries praised the outstanding functionality of the building, with its huge sorting room and its underground connection to the main railway station across the street. The ornate ironwork and the cubist window, which came from glass artist Jacques Gruber, as well as the cement sculptures on the facade, are among the most noteworthy details of the building.

Together with the Église Sainte-Jeanne-d'Arc and the Palais de la Méditerranée casino, the Poste Thiers is one of the most prominent Art Deco buildings in the city. All three are impressive architectural relics of the 1920s and 1930s, a period when Nice prospered greatly and expanded far to the north.

Address 21 Avenue Thiers, 06000 Nice | **Public transit** Tramway Gare Thiers | **Hours** Mon–Fri 8am–7pm, Sat 8am–12:30pm | **Tip** If you want, you can easily have letters or small packages sent in care of general delivery, then pick them up within 15 days at the *Poste-Restante* window with an ID card or passport. The Au Voyageur Nisart is a traditional restaurant close to the train station at 19 Rue d'Alsace-Lorraine (Tue–Sun, Tel 0033/(0)493821960, www.voyageurnissart.com).

61__Promenade du Paillon

Water games above the riverbed

The long Promenade des Anglais is world famous. Often praised, painted, and photographed, it is the hallmark of the city on the Bay of Angels. It has taken nearly 200 years, but now the renowned spot for upscale shopping and strolling has some competition in the Promenade du Paillon.

The Paillon is a river about 25 miles long flowing through the northwestern part of the old city, its source lying more than 4,000 feet up in the hills above the French Riviera. In the summer months, it is not much more than a trickle, but it can swell in the spring and after heavy rains can become a mighty stream, whose floods were feared during the Middle Ages.

After the Paillon flooded and destroyed Nice numerous times, people began to dyke the river in various construction phases and, ultimately, to build over it in the late 1800s. In a way Nice benefited from this, as the old and new cities were connected more closely together, but at the same time the Paillon disappeared from the city's collective memory. Only after the demolition of the old bus depot and a parking garage did city leaders seek a new urban design concept, and a decision was made to make the river once again "visible" through a promenade symbolic of the subterranean course of the Paillon.

When the Promenade du Paillon opened in 2013, enthusiasm was high. At a length of almost a mile, the promenade has developed into a true oasis in the heart of the city, enjoyed equally by tourists and locals. Two water features, one smaller pool and the other a gigantic 32,000-square-foot reflecting pool, are especially popular. At regular intervals, water fountains are shot high in the air for the summertime enjoyment of children. Shaded walkways welcome those out for a stroll, and numerous benches and swivel chairs invite people to relax and enjoy the scenery.

Address Promenade du Paillon, 06000 Nice | **Public transit** Tramway Masséna | **Hours** Daily 7am–11pm; in winter until 9pm | **Tip** From the roof terrace of the Musée d'Art Moderne et d'Art Contemporain, you have a magnificent view of the Promenade du Paillon and the roofs of the old town.

62__Sainte-Jeanne-d'Arc

A white wedding cake made of reinforced concrete

The Russian Orthodox Cathedral of Nice, with its onion domes, and the Cathédrale Sainte-Réparte in the historic old city are both known by visitors from around the world. But has anyone ever heard of the Église Sainte-Jeanne-d'Arc? Even the majority of art historians will shrug their shoulders, but the church lying in the north of Nice is an architectural gem.

In 1913, construction began on the Catholic house of worship, but due to the outbreak of World War I, work did not progress past the crypt. Only in 1926 did construction resume according to the plans of Jacques Droz, and the church was finally completed in 1933. The Église Sainte-Jeanne-d'Arc is considered the masterpiece of the Parisian architect; it was classified as a *Monument historique* and even appointed by the Ministry of Education and Cultural Affairs to the *Patrimoine du XXe siècle* in 2009.

Jacques Droz had the religious building constructed in reinforced concrete, influenced by the language of forms found in the Art Deco style, but he also borrowed from Gaudi, and African elements can be identified. Eleven egg-shaped domes – eight small ones and three more-imposing ones – crown the edifice, which is flanked by a bell tower with an openwork spire, the twisted shape of which symbolizes an Easter candle. A grandiose spatial effect is achieved thanks to the ellipsoidal domes. The wall paintings in the interior are by Eugène Klementieff and were clearly inspired by Russian Cubism. The stations of the cross are thematically displayed, in addition to a tapestry that describes the covenant between God and his people.

The modern design does not enjoy universal approval, however: critics compare the church, with its conspicuous white color and dome shapes, to a meringue topping, sarcastically calling it *Notre-Dame-des-Oeufs* (Our Lady of the Eggs).

Address 11 Rue Grammont, 06100 Nice | **Public transit** Bus line 23 to the Bella Vista stop or Tramway to Borriglione | **Hours** Daily 9am–6pm, tours Tue 11:00am | **Tip** The Musée National Message Biblique Marc Chagall on Avenue du Docteur Ménard is a 10-minute walk away (May–Oct, Mon, Wed–Sun 10am–6pm; Nov–Apr, Mon, Wed–Sun 10am–5pm, www.musee-chagall.fr).

63__ The Staircase

Hidden Baroque splendor

The Palais Lascaris is tucked away in a narrow street in the old city of Nice. All too often people walk right past the house, as its rather plain facade does not correspond to the great opulence of the furnishings concealed inside. Far more than other buildings in the old city, the palace is reminiscent of that glorious era of Nice that came to an abrupt end with the French Revolution.

During the Baroque era, distinguished civil and noble families had houses built in the city that were representative of the times. As space was limited in the old city of Nice, the prestige of these palaces was not often apparent from the outside, but rather in their interiors, whose immensely elegant and entertaining spaces amazed visitors.

Unfortunately, very few of these palaces are open to the public, but a notable exception is the Palais Lascaris. The palace was built beginning in 1643 by the eponymous family Lascaris-Vintimille. Modeled on the palaces of Genoa, no expense or effort was spared to highlight the family's social status, including the prominent family crest in the entry hall. During the Revolution, the house was occupied, then later converted into an apartment building, after which it was left to decay for a long period, until the city of Nice acquired it in 1942.

Following an extensive renovation, the palace was opened to the public. The monumental staircase with its marble balustrades, pillars, and sculptures, as well as the richly vaulted ceiling decorated with frescoes, are especially impressive. Accompanied by angels, you climb the steps up to the staterooms, which are decorated with atlases, caryatids, and putti, and with precious tapestries. For the last few years, a collection of historical musical instruments has been housed in one part of the building.

Address 15 Rue Droite, 06300 Nice | **Public transit** Tramway Cathédrale Vieille Ville | **Hours** Mon, Wed–Sun 10am–6pm, closed in Nov | **Tip** The ground floor of the city palace houses a historic pharmacy, which has decorations stemming from the mid-18th century.

64_ Victorine Studios
Little Hollywood on the French Riviera

As a movie set, the South of France long ago secured its place in the history of cinema. In 1895, the Lumière brothers filmed *L'Entrée du Train en Gare de La Ciotat*, or *The Arrival of a Train at La Ciotat Station*, and their spectacular pictures helped break through what was then the brand-new medium of film. Subsequently, in the 1920s, came the first movie studios in Marseille and Nice, which quickly acquired an excellent reputation, similar to the production companies in Berlin during the Weimar Republic.

In 1925, Hollywood producer Rex Ingram purchased the Victorine Film Studios in Nice and shot *Mare Nostrum*, an espionage film about German U-boats. In the following years a number of renowned movies were produced in these studios. Even after the outbreak of war, directors continued to film: in 1945, the Marcel Carné classic *Les Enfants du Paradis* (*Children of Paradise*) was created at Victorine Studios, starring Arletty and the unforgettable Jean-Louis Barrault.

After the end of World War II, the heyday of the studio began, with the filming here of such famous movies as *To Catch a Thief* with Grace Kelly and Cary Grant (1954) and *And God Created Woman* in 1956, which helped in the breakthrough of a young actress named Brigitte Bardot. From Elizabeth Taylor and Katherine Hepburn to Roger Moore, Louis de Funès, and Alain Delon, there was hardly a film star of the era who was not in front of the camera in Nice. Even cult director François Truffaut shot *Mississippi Mermaid* and *Day for Night* here.

In 1999, the Victorine Film Studios began operating under the name Studios Riviera. Covering an area of more than 750,000 square feet, 10 studios decked out with the latest technology are available to film producers, who, these days, mostly use them to shoot TV programs and commercials.

Address 16 Avenue Édouard Grinda, 06200 Nice, www.studios-riviera.com | **Getting there** The film studios are located to the west of the city center about a half mile away from the airport. | **Tip** In close proximity to the studios, at 405 Promenade des Anglais, you'll find the Musée des Arts Asiatiques, which provides fascinating insights into Chinese, Japanese, Korean, Cambodian, and Indian art (www.arts-asiatiques.com).

65_ Villa Speranza

Where Nietzsche wrote with blue fingers

Friedrich Nietzsche is counted among the many northern Europeans who spent the winter months on the French Riviera. Between 1883 and 1888. The philosopher came to Nice every winter, "to cure [his] head from suffering exclusively with pure heaven." Here in the mild climate he wrote large portions of some of his most famous works, including *Beyond Good and Evil*, *The Will to Power*, and *The Antichrist*.

Nietzsche praised the local weather as "the most invigorating climate that can be imagined," and wrote to his friend Heinrich Köselitz in Venice: "Nice, as a French city, is intolerable to me and almost a hamlet in this southern splendor; but it is also still an Italian city – and I have taken rooms there in the older part of town, and when something must be said, it is said in Italian: it is as though I am in a suburb of Genoa."

Nietzsche lived for the most part in simple guesthouses, where he was often forced for monetary reasons to make do with the cheaper north-facing rooms. From October 1886 to April 1887, he resided in the Villa Speranza on the Rue des Ponchettes under Castle Hill. It was a cold winter, and Nietzsche complained about his "blue fingers," which made it difficult for him to write: "The things I have frozen in the seven winters of my existence in the south!"

Nietzsche lived mostly withdrawn from the community. He maintained close contact neither with his housemates nor with the locals. He often took walks up to Castle Hill or excursions into the surrounding countryside. He especially loved the hike from Èze-sur-Mer up to Èze. Though sweat-inducing, it also proved inspiring: Nietzsche is said to have written several paragraphs of the famous *Thus Spoke Zarathustra* on the "arduous ascent from the station to the wonderful Moorish rocky nest of Èze."

Address 17 Rue des Ponchettes, 06300 Nice | **Public transit** Opéra Vieille Ville | **Tip** The Terrasse Frédéric Nietzsche, a viewing platform at the end of Montée Eberlé, is named for the writer.

66__ The Underwater Trail
A walk along the sea floor

Port-Cros is truly a dream island. Until 1963, it was privately owned and therefore remained virtually uninhabited. Marceline and Marcel Henry bequeathed the island to the French government on the condition that they turn its 1,705 acres into a nature reserve. The government accepted the offer, and President Pompidou ordered by decree the establishment of the Parc National de Port-Cros that same year. The special thing about Port-Cros is that the protected zone of this smallest of the French national parks stretches not only over solid ground, but also into the surrounding sea.

With its crystal clear water, the island is a popular destination for divers and snorkelers. Underwater hunting, however, is strictly forbidden, as the protection of the island's complex ecosystem is top priority. In order to raise awareness of its subaquatic flora and fauna, France's first underwater nature trail was created in Port-Cros National Park at the end of the 1980s.

The Plage de la Palud, lying directly on the north coast of the island, marks the beginning of this path, which leads to a striking, towering rock formation in the sea, the Rocher du Rascas. On the trail, whose nearly 1,000 feet are signposted with plastic panels from mid-June to mid-September, you can explore a magnificent underwater world with your snorkel and mask. Air tanks are not required, as the trail runs only a few feet below the water's surface, though fins are quite useful if you're looking to complete the course in a half hour.

Staying on course is typically not a problem, as the boards are marked by yellow buoys and are thus very easy to find. In the mysterious silence of the sea, you glide along through a shimmering carpet of sea grass. The pictures on the panels help you to identify conger, scorpion fish, grouper, and other sea creatures.

LES ROCHES ÉCLAIRÉES

Ce milieu est d'une grande richesse car la lumière favorise le développement des algues, premiers maillons de nombreuses chaînes alimentaires.

Serran écriture

Girelle paon

Girelle commune

Femelle

mâle

Chapon

Rascasse brune

Étoile de mer

Address Port-Cros, 83400 Hyères | **Getting there** Port-Cros is one of the Îles d'Hyères and can be reached by ferry several times a day from the mainland (La Tour-Fondue) during the summer. For information about connections and pricing, visit www.tlv-tvm.com. | **Tip** The neighboring island of Île du Levant, with its beautiful beaches, has been considered a nudist paradise since 1931.

67__ Venice on the Riviera

An artificially created lagoon city

The 1960s were the golden age of tourism on the French Riviera. All along the coast, new resorts and vacation homes were built. In some places, such as in La Grande-Motte or in Marina Baie des Anges, a modernist "Holiday machine" was created that could accommodate several thousand tourists simultaneously. Those who demonize these buildings today should not forget that at the time they were constructed, the environmental movement was still in its infancy and policymakers saw no other way to manage the massive influx of people.

In search of new land to build upon, Alsatian architect and contractor François Spoerry discovered a desolate stretch of coastline lying at an acute angle to the Bay of St. Tropez, upon which only the mosquitos had yet laid claim. The marshland in the Giscle Estuary was drained, and the mosquitoes, as was customary at the time, were fought using chemicals. Then in the summer of 1966, the construction of the Venice of Provence began.

Spoerry spared no effort in the design of his planned resort city. He devised a pedestrian paradise with cobblestone streets, shaded colonnades, and cantilevered bridges that connected the residential islands. A "fortified church" with the typical Provençal buttresses could not be left out any more than a town hall and marketplace. Within three decades, a considerable lagoon city had been built. The town, which long ago developed a patina, consists of more than 2,000 pastel-colored houses and a nearly 4.5-mile canal system, allowing every homeowner to have his or her own yacht mooring.

François Spoerry's project was not without controversy, but Port-Grimaud is today considered a successful example of a post-modern vacation resort and has not only been imitated internationally, but was even appointed to the *Patrimoine du XXe siècle*.

Address 83310 Port Grimaud, www.port-grimaud.fr | **Getting there** Port Grimaud is located 4.5 miles west of St. Tropez on the coastal road D 559. | **Tip** Incidentally, Port Grimaud has a very beautiful, clean, sandy beach, which was artificially created. In the eponymous old village of Grimaud, you can admire the ruins of a castle.

68___A Woman in Chains

Maillol's monument to Louis-Auguste Blanqui

Louis-Auguste Blanqui was probably already a restless soul back in his school days, giving his teachers no end of grief. But this is just speculation. One thing is certain: born the son of a sub-prefect on February 7, 1805, in Puget-Thenièrs in the Maritime Alps, Blanqui became a professional revolutionary who committed his life to social justice, taking part in numerous uprisings around the country.

Since 1908, sculptor Aristide Maillol's monumental bronze memorial has stood at the edge of the city recalling the town's famous son, who spent many years in prison. Maillol gave his monument the deeply symbolic title *L'Action Enchaînée*, which translates loosely to "the action in chains."

Blanqui was born too late to take part in the French Revolution (1789); otherwise, he would certainly have been among the rebels in the barricades. But in all the other famous uprisings of his time, be it the July Revolution of 1830, the June Days Uprising of 1848, or the Paris Commune of 1870-71, Blanqui always played a decisive role. At the Paris Commune he even served for a short time as the head of the interim government. Many of these engagements, however, did not go quite so well for him: Blanqui had to spend nearly half of his 76 years of life either in prison or in exile in Belgium. His nine years of detention in Mont-Saint-Michel were especially difficult. Blanqui's revolutionary spirit was not broken, however: his ideas and writings have had great influence over later socialist and communist movements.

There is no doubt this man deserved a monument. However, two questions about the statue remain unanswered: Why did Aristide Maillol choose to depict not a man, but rather a naked, young, athletic female with a powerfully striding gait? And why was the memorial placed right on the playground of Puget-Théniers?

Address 06260 Puget-Thenièrs | **Getting there** Puget-Thenièrs lies in the valley of the Var on the D 6202 about 45 miles from Nice. | **Tip** Puget-Thenièrs can be easily reached from Nice via the Train des Pignes (www.trainprovence.com).

69_Le Club 55

The mother of all beach clubs

In the beginning there was just a beach. A golden, solitary, sandy beach, undeveloped and isolated. Bernard de Colmont camped here with his family and loved the simple life à la Robinson Crusoe. Then Bernard received a modest inheritance and used it in 1953 to buy a small piece of land behind the dunes on the Plage de Pampelonne. Together with his wife, he built a simple wooden hut, lacking both water and electricity, but they enjoyed the summer months there and cooked for the few friends who popped in for a visit.

Two years later, the director Roger Vadim was driving by in his jeep and asked if they could entertain his film crew, who were nearby shooting a movie called *And God Created Woman*. With that, Le Club 55 was born. Madame de Colmont put some freshly caught sardines on the grill, and Brigitte Bardot and Françoise Sagan were among their first guests that fateful day.

The *Cinquante-Cinq*, with its unique ambiance, is regarded today as the mother of all beach clubs. The atmosphere is relaxed, and visitors aren't treated like kings but as friends. There has been a steady stream of stars through the club's doors ever since it opened and the guest list is more than remarkable: it ranges from Gunter Sachs and Alain Delon to François Mitterrand and Mikhail Gorbachev, and all the way to Bill Gates, George Clooney, and Bono. The latter performed a legendary spontaneous concert a few years ago with U2 that brought the entire club to a halt.

As a rule, you'll need a reservation to get in. That is, unless your name is Bruce Willis or Karl Lagerfeld. Seats at the white tables are in high demand, and the food is simple but very good. Classic dishes include the Provençal vegetable platter and the grilled *loup de mer*. Instead of champagne, the drink of choice is a delightful rosé from the owners' vineyards.

Address 43 Boulevard Patch, 83550 Ramatuelle, Tel 0033/(0)494555555, www.club55.fr | **Getting there** The Boulevard Patch branches off to the east from the Route des Plages (D 93), which runs between St. Tropez and Ramatuelle. | **Hours** Mar 20 – Nov 5 and between Christmas and New Year, daily 11am – 6pm | **Tip** One almost forgets that the Club 55 also claims its own stretch of beach. Upholstered sun loungers are available for rent so you can sunbathe in style.

70__Ferme Ladouceur
Tables in the vineyard

The peninsula of St. Tropez is known throughout the world primarily as a playground for the rich and famous. Numerous celebrities, such as fashion mogul Daniel Hechter and soccer official Michel Platin, own large estates typical of the area. But St. Tropez also has its rural side, where the vineyards extend down to the sea between the mountain villages of Gassin and Ramatuelle. The varietal that is mainly grown here, the Côtes de Provence, produces an excellent rosé with a bright color as well as fine fruity and subtle floral accents.

Among the traditional wineries scattered across the peninsula stands the Ferme Ladouceur, housed in a dreamy country estate also known in the South of France as a *bastide*, from the late 19th century. It was acquired in 1910 by Eugène Ladouceur and has remained a family-owned enterprise ever since. About three decades ago, the family decided not only to grow wine grapes, but also to entertain guests on their property and to showcase the culinary delicacies of Provence. These days, you can sit on the large terrace behind the house when the weather is nice, surrounded by olive and fig trees and the property's vineyards. The atmosphere is casual, and the cooking is usually down to earth, though at times tinged with Asian accents. Delectable appetizers that have been offered include yellow beets with summer truffles or a poached egg with chorizo. Appealing main courses include a cassolette of monkfish and a rack of lamb cooked *à point*.

Only a single, prix-fixe three-course meal is served, which changes daily, along with a bottle of delicious house wine of your choice: red, rosé, or white. As the bottle of wine is bottomless, it is definitely a good idea to decide upon a designated driver for the trip home before sitting down to eat …

Address Quartier La Rouillère, 83550 Ramatuelle, Tel 0033/(0)494792495, www.fermeladouceur.com | **Getting there** Below the town, drive in the direction of St. Tropez, then turn right onto the D 61. Ferme Ladouceur will be on the left-hand side after about two miles. | **Hours** Mar–Dec, only open in the evening | **Tip** There are also several attractive guest rooms available in the bastide. Another good restaurant nearby is La Verdoyante at 866 Avenue de Coste Bugade (Tel 0033/(0)494561623, www.la-verdoyante.fr).

71_Domaine du Rayol
A global garden

Every Provençal city has its municipal park and every townhouse has its own small garden, but most of them lack that certain *je ne sais quoi,* the little something that sets a garden apart and turns a simple green space into an enchanted mini paradise. This is not the case with the Domaine du Rayol, which offers a very unique tribute to the landscapes of the Mediterranean. And although it's undoubtedly one of the most beautiful gardens on the French Riviera, it is fortunately also still a secret to the uninitiated.

This difficult-to-access section of the coastline had long been under private ownership. A banker named Alfred Courmes had a magnificent Art Deco villa built here in 1910, which was later purchased by the aircraft engineer Henri Potez, who temporarily employed nearly a dozen gardeners in his park. But after World War II, the garden became increasingly overgrown, and only when the Coastal Protection Agency, or Conservatoire du Littoral, acquired the nearly 50-acre site in 1989 did the Domaine du Rayol literally blossom into life. Under the overall leadership of Gilles Clément, a talented landscape architect, the land lying directly along the ocean was imaginatively replanted according to various design principles.

The main axis of the gardens is a staircase lined by cypresses and a small forest of holm oak trees. Terraces dominate across the hillsides, linked by enchanting pathways. Though they grow under the same climatic conditions, each area of plantings has their origins on different continents. In the Mexican garden, yucca, agave, and cacti bloom; in the Canary Islands garden, there are delightful echium and dragon trees. Australia is represented by eucalyptus and acacia, New Zealand by tree ferns, and South Africa by a large thorny hawthorn.

Address Avenue des Bèlges, 83820 Rayol-Canadel-sur-Mer, www.domainedurayol.org |
Getting there Le Rayol is between Hyères and St. Tropez; from the coastal road (D 559),
signs lead to the Domaine. | **Hours** Apr–June and Sep–mid-Nov, daily 9:30am–6:30pm;
July–Aug, daily 9:30am–7:30pm; in winter, daily 9:30am–5pm | **Tip** In July and August,
special beach explorations for families and children are offered weekdays at 10:30am
(reservations can be made by calling Tel 0033/(0)498044400).

72__Le Corbusier's Grave

A view of the sea for eternity

The world-renowned architect and urban planner Le Corbusier, whose real name was actually Charles Édouard Jeanneret, had already become familiar with Roquebrune and Cap Martin at the end of the 1920s, when he visited the designer Eileen Gray, who had built a summer house on the coast here. Le Corbusier fell in love with the stretch of coastline and henceforth traveled almost every August to the French Riviera to spend his holidays.

After purchasing a coveted hillside property on the sea in 1951, he designed for himself and his wife a simple wooden *cabanon* – or vacation cottage – following his Modulor scale of proportions, on a footprint of only 12 feet by 12 feet, which was integrated perfectly into the landscape. The Le Corbusier house is especially exciting for architecture lovers, with its spartan yet well thought out built-in furnishings, all made by the architect himself. It would have been understandable for Corbusier's wife, however, to complain about the lack of comfort – there is only a single narrow bed in the tiny cabin, for instance.

On August 27, 1967, Le Corbusier died near his home after suffering a heart attack while diving. He was laid to rest in the Cimetière Saint-Pancrace in Roquebrune, where other prominent personalities, including the poet William Butler Yeats, the Russian Grand Duchess Xenia Alexandrovna Romanov, and the painter José Barreau have found their final resting place.

Corbusier's grave clearly stands out from the others because, as befits an architect of his rank and stature, he designed the tomb himself in 1958 after the death of his wife, Yvonne, and chose a location with a view of the sea. It is as simple as his *cabanon*. The gravestone is dominated by a concrete cube, with the couple's names and dates of birth and death painted on two colorful plates.

Address Chemin de Gorbio, 06190 Roquebrune-Cap-Martin. The grave can be found on Carré H, number 3. | **Getting there** Roquebrune is about three miles east of Monaco, a half mile above the coastal road (D 6007) on the D 2564. The cemetery is a five-minute walk east of the village via the Rue de la Fontaine. | **Hours** Apr–Sep, daily 8am–6:45pm; Oct–Mar, daily 8am–4:45pm | **Tip** Every Tuesday and Friday at 9:30am a tour to Le Corbusier's *cabanon* starts at the Tourist Office, 218 Avenue Aristide-Briand (reservations required, contact the Office Municipal de Tourisme: Tel 0033/(0)493356287, www.roquebrune-cap-martin.com).

73__ The Olive Tree
A thousand-year-old root system

There is probably no other plant as emblematic of the vegetation and the culture of the Mediterranean Sea as the olive tree, or *Olea europaea*. For the English poet Lawrence Durrell, the beauty of the entire Mediterranean realm was truly reflected in the glimmer of a single black olive. First grown on the eastern shores of the Mediterranean, the olive tree was brought by the Greeks to their settlements in Italy, Sicily, and the coast of southern France. The Greek colonists cultivated extensive olive groves, as the oil was a staple of Greek cooking and the wood from the trees was used to make furniture and burned as a fuel.

Although olive cultivation no longer plays an important role in the economy of the French Riviera, Roquebrune still boasts one of the world's oldest olive trees. With a spread of over 52 feet and a height of more than 42 feet, the *olivier millénaire* stands about a tenth of a mile east of the old city on the edge of a narrow street. Its ossified root system alone is several yards wide and over the centuries has climbed the neighboring wall like a futuristic wooden sculpture. Exotic in its originality, the tree provides pleasant shade in the summer with its silvery leaves splashed here and there with blues and greens.

The olive tree of Roquebrune is estimated to be over a thousand years old, though there are some botanists who suspect it could be well over 2,000 years old. Given that an average-size olive tree produces between 150 and 220 pounds of olives annually, or nearly three gallons of oil per annum, you can calculate what a huge amount of oil the ancient Goliath has theoretically produced in its lifetime thus far.

The medieval village of Roquebrune-Cap Martin, built around a 10th-century castle, offers many beautiful views of the coastline.

Address Chemin de Menton, 06190 Roquebrune-Cap Martin | **Getting there** Roquebrune
is about three miles east of Monaco a half mile above the coastal road (D 6007) on the
D 2564. The olive tree is a five-minute walk east of the village via the Rue de la Fontaine. |
Tip From the castle of Roquebrune, which is probably younger than the *olivier millénaire*,
you'll have a wonderful view of the coast and the Cap Martin (Jun–Sep, daily 10am–1pm
and 2:30–7pm; Oct–Jan to 5pm; Feb–May until 6pm).

74_ Villa E.1027

Une maison charmante!

Eileen Gray is one of the most important designers of the 20th century. Her designs for tables and lamps, executed in steel tubes and glass, are considered modern classics. Often reproduced by copycats, the originals have fetched prices in the millions at Christie's, the prestigious international auction house.

It is less well known, however, that Gray also worked as an architect. Only three of her designs were built, all houses in which she lived during different periods of her life. The most famous of these is the Villa E.1027, which Gray realized between 1926 and 1929 at Cap Martin. Its mysterious name, E.1027, was composed from abbreviations: *E* is for Eileen and the numbers 10, 2, and 7 stand for the numerical positions in the alphabet of the initials of her then-lover, Jean Badovici (10=J, 2=B), and the 7 for the G in Gray. The white L-shaped, flat-roofed building with floor-to-ceiling windows is considered in itself a complete work of modernist art, congenially tying together nature and architecture.

"*Une maison charmant!*" exclaimed the architect Le Corbusier about the vacation home of his friend, which was perched just above the craggy rocks, its form clearly reminiscent of a ship. (Le Corbusier painted a number of murals throughout the house during a long visit.) Although Gray and Badovici separated in the early 1930s, she left the forward-looking villa to her former lover.

A later heir to Badovici sold the furnishings after his death, and the Villa E.1027 was eventually left to decay over the years. Vandalism raged, the concrete crumbled, cracks crawled up the walls, the grilles and window frames rusted. Fortunately, the house was acquired by the Conservatoire du Littoral just in time and was carefully renovated. The villa should soon be accessible to the public.

Address Plage de Buse, 06190 Roquebrune-Cap-Martin | **Getting there** Cap Martin is about three miles east of Monaco along the coastal road (D 6007). From the train station, the house is only a 5-minute walk east. | **Tip** The Promenade Le Corbusier leads right above the Villa E.1027. On this beautiful coastal path you can walk around Cap Martin.

75__ The Border Train Station

More like a castle than a stationhouse

Who, among us, is not familiar with the small, secluded provincial train stations? A train only comes a few times a day, and if you're lucky there will be a small stationhouse or at least a roof to provide a bit of shade and protection if bad weather strikes while you wait.

Those who arrive at Saint-Dalmas-de-Tende by rail with similar expectations will be surprised by the abnormally large stationhouse, which would better suit a city such as Nice, and looks noticeably out of place in this small village. In fact, you could probably fit all the residents of Saint-Dalmas inside the building at once and have plenty of room to spare!

Saint-Dalmas-de-Tende, at an altitude of nearly 2,300 feet above sea level, is a stop on the Tenda Railway (see p. 18), which leads from Nice through Sospel and into the Italian town of Cuneo. Construction began in 1910, and countless viaducts and tunnels had to be built for the railroad to be able to cross the rugged Maritime Alps.

The station of Saint-Dalmas-de-Tende was, at the time, not just any old station: it was *the* Italian border station. Before the railway line was finally put into operation in October 1928, Mussolini had this monumental structure – which is reminiscent of a two-winged castle – built in the town then known as San Dalmazzo. Until 1947, the border between France and Italy went right through the upper Roya Valley. Only through a referendum, in which the higher standard of living in France played the deciding role, was San Dalmazzo renamed Saint-Dalmas and turned over to the French. In the local dialect, however, the Italian roots live on to this day.

The railway line and the station of Saint-Dalmas were damaged during World War II. While the Tenda Railway restored its connection to Cuneo in 1979, the oversized building continues to decay.

Address 06430 Saint-Dalmas-de-Tende | **Getting there** Saint-Dalmas-de-Tende is located in the Roya Valley, about 25 miles from the coast on the E 74. | **Tip** A small road (D 91) winds from the station up to Lac des Mèches, about 1,280 feet above sea level. The reservoir is a good starting point for exploring the Mercantour National Park and the rock carvings in the Vallée des Merveilles.

76__The Fort

The southernmost point of the Maginot Line

Perched on a mountaintop like an eagle's nest at an elevation of 2,500 feet, Sainte-Agnès is not merely one of the most beautiful places in France; this mountain village located on a spur of the Maritime Alps is also regarded as the highest-lying coastal village in Europe. Although just a couple of miles from the Mediterranean, it takes even experienced hikers at least two very sweaty hours to reach the medieval settlement from Menton.

French military strategists in the twentieth century were also keenly aware of the unique location of Sainte-Agnès when they began to secure borders to deter and repel attacks from neighbors along their eastern flank. This defensive line, part of a mighty fortification system consisting of bunkers and casemates, was named after former French minister of defense André Maginot.

From 1931 to 1934, Sainte-Agnès was built out as the southernmost point of the Maginot Line. On the southern edge of the village, the powerful gun bastions of the fort are still grounded deep into the rock, where they were drilled down to a depth of 180 feet. Up to 300 soldiers could be housed at any time in the completely self-sufficient fortress; in the underground complex there were not only kitchens and bedrooms, but also a hospital with an operating room.

In June 1940, the worst-case scenario played out: as Mussolini's troops began to cross the French border, they were fired on from Fort Sainte-Agnès and forced to retreat. Ultimately, though, the defensive system could not prevent French capitulation.

The fortifications were actively used by the military until 1990. Only then was the fortress handed over to the town government of Sainte-Agnès, which opened the site as a museum for visitors. So today, you can explore the fort on your own.

Address Avenue du Château, 06500 Sainte-Agnès | **Getting there** Sainte-Agnès is reached from Menton via the D 22; the fort is located at the end of the cul-de-sac. | **Hours** June–Sep, daily 10:30am–12pm and 3–7pm; Oct–May, Sat and Sun 2:30–5:30pm | **Tip** The restaurant Le Righi in Sainte-Agnès is known not only for its great panoramic terrace, but also for its fresh homemade pasta (closed on Wed, Tel 0033/(0)492109088, www.restaurant-lerighi.fr).

77 _ The Leopold II Monument
The Butcher of the Congo

The noble peninsula of Cap Ferrat remained largely untouched by civilization until well into the 19th century. Among the first celebrities who settled on the headland were Béatrice de Rothschild, the art collector from the infamous family, and Leopold II, the king of Belgium. The monarch acquired a vast tract of land and had a splendid villa built, which once again made headlines in 2010, when a Russian oligarch made an offer to buy it for €390 million. If that price seems awfully steep for a summer home, consider that it did not even include the entirety of the royal estate as it stood in Leopold's time. The largest part of the property is parkland, and the villas of his three mistresses and the domicile for his confessor are no longer up for sale.

Leopold loved the French Riviera. It was not just the Mediterranean landscape and sea that the Belgian king was so enamored of – he also developed a pretty severe gambling habit and appreciated the close proximity to the Casino of Monte Carlo. Leopold had plenty of money to play with, because since 1885 his private portfolio included the Congo in central Africa, which he exploited ruthlessly until his death. The Congolese were subjugated and abused for decades – tortured, mutilated, and murdered. Current reputable historical estimates infer that Leopold's colonial rule claimed around 10 million lives, cutting the population of the Congo in half.

Oddly enough, *Quelcues Amis de la Côte d'Azur* came together in 1911 to erect a monument in the middle of the peninsula to their royal friend, who had died two years earlier, and it still stands by the roadside today. A bronze portrait in half profile shows the "Butcher of the Congo" with his beard, which, incidentally, he always stuffed into a special rubber cover while swimming in the sea to protect it from the water.

A
MEMOIRE
S BELGES
LD II
RRAT

there
the

78_Villa Santo Sospir

The tattooed house

The peninsula of Cap Ferrat is one of the most prestigious locations along the French Riviera: distinguished stylishness behind unfriendly high walls. The Villa Ephrussi de Rothschild and its famous gardens stand on the peninsula's narrow isthmus, which is only a few hundred meters wide. While travelers crowd before its gates, there are only a handful of tourists aware of the Villa Santo Sospir, which is hidden nearby.

The patroness Francine Weisweiller lived in this relatively unknown gem on the southwestern edge of the peninsula. She was a close friend of Jean Cocteau and repeatedly supported him in his film projects. After Cocteau finished the strenuous work of filming *Les Enfants Terribles*, she invited him to her villa on Cap Ferrat, in May of 1950, so that he could relax and recuperate. They enjoyed a carefree summer together; Jean Marais stopped by, and they all took sailing trips along the coast when the sun was shining.

But after a relatively short time, Cocteau began to get bored and asked Francine if he could paint the wall above her fireplace. Spurred on by the enthusiasm of his hostess, he let his creativity run wild, and overlaid almost all the walls of the villa with a potpourri of frescoes, mosaics, and erotically charged interior decorations. Cocteau was pleased: "Santo Sospir is a tattooed villa." The artist remained a welcome guest at Cap Ferrat – he also filmed *La Villa Santo Sospir* here, as well as scenes for *Testament of Orpheus*.

The Villa Santo Sospir, still owned by the Weisweiller family, has long enjoyed protected status as a monument and can be visited by anyone interested in diving into the world of Cocteau. The villa's doors open to a Mediterranean fantasy world filled with mythological scenes and characters, which have an appeal that is just as strong today as it was back then.

Address 14 Avenue Jean Cocteau, 06230 Saint-Jean-Cap-Ferrat, www.villasantosospir.fr |
Getting there Saint-Jean-Cap-Ferrat is just over four miles east of Nice. The D 125 leads
directly to the Cap Ferrat. The villa is on the southwestern tip of the peninsula. | **Hours**
Open daily by appointment only (Tel 0033/(0)493760016) | **Tip** If you are up for it, you
can walk around the entire peninsula in about three hours on a coastal trail. It is best to
start at the Plage de Passable and follow the Chemin du Roy (King's Road) south.

79__ The Memorial Plaque

Remembering an exodus

Saint-Martin-de-Vésubie is a peaceful village high in the French Maritime Alps. Surrounded by stunning mountain panoramas, it is all too easy to forget the tragedies that happened here during World War II.

Like the rest of the Département Alpes-Maritimes, Saint-Martin-de-Vésubie at that time also belonged to the Italian occupation zone of France, so the Jews living there enjoyed a certain degree of protection against the Germans. The Italians did force the Jews to live in specific areas, but they refused to send them to the concentration camps despite repeated German protests.

After the armistice with Italy was signed, however, the situation changed abruptly. The Jews realized that they were trapped, and on September 8, 1943, many decided to seek refuge by fleeing. Around a thousand Jews, including pregnant women, children, and several elderly men and women, tried desperately to get from Saint-Martin-de-Vésubie over the Alps along old mule tracks to Piedmont, in Italy. Unfortunately, Italy, too, was to become unsafe when, just four days later, on September 12, German troops invaded there. With the help of the local population, the majority of the refugees succeeded in escaping the Nazis' clutches, but nearly 350 were arrested by the SS and interned in Borgo San Dalmazzo. The prisoners were then all deported through the stations in Drancy and Nice to the Auschwitz-Birkenau concentration camp, where all but 10 were murdered.

Decades later, memorial plaques were installed in Saint-Martin-de-Vésubie and on the Col de Fenestre to commemorate the "biblical exodus." In 2010, two police officers and their wives were also posthumously awarded the honorary titles of "Righteous Among the Nations" because, despite the danger, they had hidden two Jewish infants from the Nazis in the gendarmerie.

Address Route de la Vésubie, 06450 Saint-Martin-de-Vésubie | **Getting there**
Saint-Martin-de-Vésubie is about 40 miles north of Nice on the D 2565. The memorial is
located about 500 feet from the center of town on the right-hand side. | **Tip** Every year on
September 9, commemorative walks are organized along the historic route, and many
people take part.

ICI UN MILLIER DE JUIFS
HOMMES FEMMES ENFANTS VIEILLARDS
AIDES PAR LES ORGANISATIONS JUIVES
PROTÉGÉS PAR L'ARMÉE ITALIENNE D'OCCUPATION
ONT CONNU UN REPIT JUSQU'AU 8 SEPTEMBRE 1943
JOUR OÙ S'EST DÉCHAINÉE LA HAINE RACIALE
DE L'OCCUPANT ALLEMAND

FRANCHISSANT
LES MONTAGNES DANS UN 'EXODE BIBLIQUE'
350 D'ENTRE EUX FURENT REPRIS PAR LES SS
ET INTERNÉS À BORGO SAN DALMAZZO
TRANSFÉRÉS PAR LA GESTAPO
DE NICE SUR DRANCY
ILS FURENT DÉPORTÉS AU CAMP DE LA MORT
D'AUSCHWITZ-BIRKENAU
OÙ PRESQUE TOUS FURENT EXTERMINÉS

SOUVENONS-NOUS DE CES VICTIMES INNOCENTES
CRUAUTÉ DE LEURS BOURREAUX
HUMANITÉ DE CEUX

80_ Bazar Mercerie

Beach pails instead of jewels

St. Tropez is a mecca for the rich and famous. Some of those who stroll along the harborfront esplanade sport watches and jewelry whose prices are easily on par with the entire annual salary of a middle-class worker. There is hardly a luxury brand that is not represented by a shop in St. Tropez. In just a handful of streets, the storefronts of Cartier, Prada, Chanel, Hermès, Gucci, and Dior all line up one after another. After all, who knows when you might have to quickly run out before dinner to pick up a Louis Vuitton bag or a pair of Prada sandals? In St. Tropez, no desire remains unfulfilled – provided you have the means.

Is all of St. Tropez in the hands of luxury brands? No, there is at least one small business that manages a sympathetic and embittered resistance: in the middle of the Rue Gambetta you'll find the Bazar Mercerie, an ancient shop that still retains the air of times long past. "Chez Eugenie" is written in curly letters on the Bordeaux-red facade, and the stands out front are overflowing with miniature cars, colorful beach toys, and baskets, while cheap plastic balls dangle in nets overhead.

The Bazar Mercerie was opened shortly before World War II by the grandmother of the current owner, Eugenie. For more than 75 years, children's dreams have come true here. In the glorious mess you can still find innumerable outdated board games and an unimaginable number of ancient action figures. With its prime location, it is no wonder that several investors with thick checkbooks have come calling, but Eugenie has so far turned down all these lucrative offers and chosen instead to safeguard one of the last authentic corners of St. Tropez from the attack of commercialism. And thus, true snobs will still be more impressed with a beach toy from Eugenie than with a Cartier watch.

Address 16 Rue Gambetta, 83990 St. Tropez | **Getting there** The Rue Gambetta is located just a few hundred feet behind the Old Port. | **Hours** Apr–Oct, daily 9am–7pm | **Tip** Le Rucher de St. Tropez, the small shop specializing in honey at 30 Rue François Sibilli, also runs a stand in the St. Tropez market (Tue and Sat).

81__ The Café-Patisserie Sénéquier

See and be seen

The Old Port of St. Tropez is, quite simply, the place to be. The most expensive and luxurious yachts are moored here, and it is obligatory for all tourists to stroll up and down at least once during their visit. It is also here that you'll see the lowest necklines and the shortest skirts.

For a front row seat to watch all the action, there is no better choice than the café Sénéquier. Located right on the waterfront promenade, its iconic red awning and red triangular tables and chairs are visible from quite a distance.

The Sénéquier is an institution in St. Tropez. Originally opened in 1887 by Marie and Martin Sénéquier as a bakery, it would later became a patisserie, and in 1930 expand into a cafe with a large outdoor terrace. It was damaged during the bombing of the port in 1944, but was reconstructed and reopened in 1948 – just in time to accompany the ascent of St. Tropez to the highest realm of society, led in its charge by Brigitte Bardot.

Patrons of the café have also included Errol Flynn, Pablo Picasso, Miles Davis, and Jean-Paul Sartre. Nevertheless, it is part of the philosophy of the Sénéquier that prominent guests are not to be disturbed and should be served like everyone else. In other words, the Sénéquier is the ideal place to relax and enjoy a café crème or aperitif and feel the pulse of St. Tropez. A cheap pleasure, however, it is not.

From the café there is still a direct accessway into the traditional patisserie, which is famous for its white and very soft nougat. It is prepared according to a secret family recipe, and only a few of its ingredients are revealed to the public: honey from Provence, almonds from Spain, and pistachios from Sicily.

Address Quai Jean Jaurès, 83990 St. Tropez. www.senequier.com | **Getting there** The cafe is located right at the Old Port. | **Hours** Apr–Sep, daily 8am–2pm; Oct–mid-Nov and mid-Dec–Mar, daily 8am–6:30pm | **Tip** You are instantly recognizable as a tourist if you enter the cafe from the patio. Locals enter discreetly via the path that runs behind the terrace.

82_ The Coastal Path

A great walking tour around the peninsula

Hiking in St. Tropez? When you first hear such an idea, it may strike you as odd, but a hike is actually the best way to get to know the peninsula and its famous beaches.

When you tire of the glamorous hustle and bustle around the famous marina of the celebrity resort town, you'll be thrilled at how quickly you can find peace and quiet along the coast and how much nature is right at your fingertips if you just know where to look. Along the coastal path, you'll find typical Mediterranean vegetation such as carnations, mallows, thistles, chicory, and wild carrots. In other words, it really is worth it to escape town for a bit and explore the peninsula on foot.

The coastal path begins directly above the Cimetière Marin and you can stop at a great beach restaurant right on the Plage des Graniers before you start. It then continues along the bay at the Plage des Canebiers. This is the beach for all you Brigitte Bardot fans, as her famous Villa La Madrague stands just a few steps away. A few small hidden coves lure visitors in around the Pointe de la Rabiou, before you reach the largely unspoiled Plage des Salins. From here, it's not far to the most famous beach of the French Riviera: the golden Plage de Pampelonne, where the rich and famous lie beneath the sun or meet up for dinner at the legendary beach restaurant, Le Club 55. The northern part of the beach is also known as the "Tahiti-Plage."

Those still not satisfied can hike even farther, to Cap Lardier. There, at the southern tip of the peninsula of St. Tropez, you will find some relatively lonely, rocky coves with crystal clear water that offer great diving and snorkeling.

With all that, the hike can easily occupy a whole day. For the return trip, we recommend relying on the services of a taxi driver.

Address 83990 St. Tropez | **Getting there** At the end of the Old Port, the yellow marked coastal path begins at the distinctive round tower (Tour du Portalet). | **Tip** Don't forget your swimsuit! Carry plenty of drinks. There is a nice beach restaurant on the Plage des Graniers (daily 12pm–11pm, www.plagedesgraniers.com).

83_ Gendarmerie Nationale

The most famous police station in France

Louis de Funès is still revered today as one of France's most beloved comedians. His trademarks were his twisted grimaces and his cantankerous attacks, which he perfected in the crime comedy *Fantomas*, and he was known even more famously as the police chief Ludovic Cruchot in *The Troops of St. Tropez*. Anyone who has ever seen one of his gendarmes films will never be able to forget the relentless shrill of Cruchot's whistle.

In 1964, the unforgettable comedian romped as the chief of police on the big screen for the first time, infamously struggling to halt imminent moral decline by enforcing the prohibition of nude sunbathing on Tahiti beach, and attempting to flag down parking violators and speeders with his wild gesticulations. Five more films followed, which not only increased the fame of de Funès, but also showcased St. Tropez's scenic harbor. Together with Brigitte Bardot, de Funès decisively helped shape the image of the ritzy port town. To this day, numerous anecdotes about the filming of these famous movies still circulate around St. Tropez. The story of the farmer from Ramatuelle, for instance, is happily and often retold: the man was so frightened at the sight of a flying saucer that he led his ducks into the harbor, where they almost drowned. Unfortunately, no one had told him they were just filming a scene from *The Troops & Aliens*.

The *gendarmerie* has long since moved, but the old buildings of the Gendarmerie Nationale that still stand in town have gained a cult following. Day after day, countless tourists have their pictures taken in front of the buildings' recently repainted sign and closed shutters. Since interest has remained strong, a museum of film history will be opened here in the near future, and France's most famous police chief will, naturally, be prominently featured.

Address Place Blanqui, 83990 St. Tropez | **Getting there** A two-minute walk from the Parking du Nouveau Port. | **Tip** Another famous film location is the picturesque Chapelle Saint-Anne, which was used as the backdrop for the wedding scenes in the movie *The Gendarme Gets Married* (original title: *Le Gendarme Se Marie*). It is located in the town of Ramatuelle, a few miles south of St. Tropez.

84__Hotel La Ponche

And God created woman

St. Tropez and Brigitte Bardot share a passionate relationship that began 60 years ago with the filming of *And God Created Woman* (*Et Dieu Créa la Femme*) and continues to this day.

It was 1955 when a young Roger Vadim shot the movie that turned Brigitte Bardot into an international star, thanks to her trademark pout, and enshrined St. Tropez forever on the tourist map. The film's success was well orchestrated: in just the second scene of the movie, we see the young Bardot nude, lolling in the sun. From there, the merriment continues as the innocent, naive orphan girl, Juliette – "B.B." – cheerfully frolics barefoot on the beach of St. Tropez, breaking men's hearts with her inimitable sex appeal and creating the mythos of herself and her defiant lips. Within just a few weeks of the film's premiere, St. Tropez had earned its new reputation as a veritable sin city, where half-naked women dance the mambo in the streets. Of course, everyone wanted to come experience this for themselves, though in reality the town was and still is quite prudish.

At that time, the Hotel La Ponche was a simple bar for fishermen in the eponymous district, whose guests included Boris Vian and Simone de Beauvoir. Above the bar there were a few modest rooms where Vadim's film crew stayed during the filming of *And God Created Woman*. For Brigitte Bardot, La Ponche was a mythical hotel, "Where we felt at once like we were at home, where Françoise Sagan, Juliette Gréco, and a whole gang of funny cronies stayed … Those were the good old days, when we were carefree, when everything was simple and honest." There's no question: Bardot had a special relationship with the hotel; it's where she also spent her first night with her future husband, Gunter Sachs. As a tribute to the actress, a suite was later named in her honor.

Address 5 Rue des Remparts, 83990 St. Tropez. Tel 0033/(0)494970253, www.laponche.com | **Getting there** The hotel is a 5-minute walk from the Old Port. The nearest parking is at Place des Lices. | **Tip** If you're a fan, you can follow in the footsteps of Bardot through St. Tropez, by sitting in her favorite bistro, Le Gorille, or by running along the Plage des Cannebiers, where her Villa La Madrague stands just a few steps behind the beach.

85__ The House of Butterflies
A visit to Maison des Papillons

When you grow tired of all the yachts, money, and crowds parading around the Old Port of St. Tropez, the Maison des Papillons is the perfect off-the-beaten path destination.

In a narrow alley near the sea, hidden behind a nondescript door, lies a fascinating and beautiful collection of butterflies, which have been hunted and preserved over the last several decades in France and around the world by the painter and passionate lepidopterist, Dany Lartigue.

Overall, Lartigue's unique collection includes more than 25,000 specimens. In addition to exotic species from Africa, the Amazon region, and Peru, you can view butterflies native to France, such as the "Black Apollo," which Lartigue has gathered from the Gorges du Verdon and the Mercantour National Park. The museum is especially fascinating because of the unusual presentation of the creatures: the butterfly display follows a trajectory that is decidedly more aesthetic than scientific. Most of the insects are arranged in all their colorful glory as collages, with the background panels set with artful scenes by Lartigue.

Because the Maison des Papillons is housed in a typical St. Tropez mansion dating from the 19th century, visitors also receive insight into the structure of a traditional house, where the biggest attraction is certainly the hidden and idyllic courtyard. In its own way, the house is also a family museum, because Dany Lartigue is the son of the famous photographer Jacques Henri Lartigue, whose pictures from speeding racecars are considered among the first snapshots ever taken. On the walls of the stairwell hang several black-and-white photographs by Lartigue – mostly summer scenes from around the Côte-d'Azur – capturing the glorious era of the 1920s and 1930s.

Address 9 Rue Etienne Berny, 83990 St. Tropez | **Getting there** Located in a narrow alley near the Old Port. | **Hours** Apr–Sep, Mon–Sat 2:30–6pm | **Tip** Housed in a chapel at the Old Port, the Musée de l'Annonciade presents works by Matisse, Seurat, Dufy, and Utrillo.

86_The Marine Cemetery
A seaside graveyard

Its location alone is a dream, you might even be tempted to say, to die for: a few minutes' walk to the southeast of town lies the Cimetière Marin of St. Tropez, which rises just a few feet above the azure blue of the Mediterranean, its crashing surf clearly audible below. During storms, the waves can even break over the walls. There is no question: this marine burial ground is one of the most atmospheric cemeteries in all of France.

The graveyard, which was created in 1791, is divided by a network of dusty, slightly sloping pathways lined by graves. *"À mon père," "à mon ami," "à mon frère,"* and other dedications can be read on the small plaques of marble and brass. Portraits of the deceased framed in medallions have been placed on some of the gravestones; memories in sepia, bleached by the sun. Many inscriptions refer to the sea and some are decorated with pictures of sailboats. Some of the stones tell the fate of sailors who drowned in the sea.

Among those who have found their final resting places here are not only sailors and members of the old established families of St. Tropez – who trace their origins to Genoese merchants – but also, for example, Blandine Liszt, a daughter of Franz Liszt; the painter André Dunoyer de Segonzac; the singer Pierre Bachelet; and the actor and director Roger Vadim, who filmed the classic *And God Created Woman* with his first wife, Brigitte Bardot, in St. Tropez. Bardot's parents also are buried here.

Especially in the late afternoon, when the sun sinks low, the white gravestones and sarcophagi offer a striking contrast against the dark blue surface of the water and create the illusion of a sort of limbo between sky and sea.

If we must spend eternity someplace on Earth, it is hard to imagine a better spot than this one.

Address Chemin des Granier, 83990 St. Tropez | **Getting there** The cemetery is located east of the city near the citadel. | **Hours** Daily 10am–6pm | **Tip** Above the cemetery sits the citadel of St. Tropez. In addition to a great view, there is an interesting permanent display about the life of seamen (Oct–Mar, daily 10am–12:30pm and 1:30–5:30pm; Apr–Sep, daily 10am–6:30pm).

87__ The Parking du Nouveau Port

Room for 1,477 sets of wheels

"St. Tropez has a population of 5,000 inhabitants and more than 5 million visitors each year," reports Claude Maniscalo, the director of the city's tourism bureau. On the one hand, this is good news for the town's economy, but on the other hand, it also means that St. Tropez is literally bursting at the seams each summer under the onslaught of tourists. On some days during the high season, up to 100,000 visitors come to the Provençal port town and jostle their way through its picturesque streets.

Back in the 1950s, the famous writer Colette noted, "A single road leads into St. Tropez. To leave the town again, you have to take the same road out. But why would you ever want to leave?" The crux is this: since visitors today typically arrive with their own vehicles, you are almost always stuck in traffic on the coastal road into and out of town. Those last couple of miles will certainly fray your nerves, because it's bumper to bumper with vacationers all summer long.

And when you finally reach St. Tropez, what most visitors see before them is not the postcard harbor with its yachts, but rather the Parking du Nouveau Port. Think of this large parking lot as the catch basin for stranded rental cars. Exactly 1,477 marked and metered parking spaces are available in an area the size of several soccer fields. Every year, St. Tropez collects more than €4 million in parking fees here! Thus, the Parking du Nouveau Port is actually the main source of revenue on the city's balance sheet.

But there are always ways to save on pesky parking fees: just arrive by boat instead. If you're not fortunate enough to have your own luxury yacht, you can cross to St. Tropez from Saint-Maxime via ferry.

Address Parking du Nouveau Port, Passage du Port, 83990 St. Tropez | **Getting there** The Parking du Nouveau Port is located close to the harbor. Take the Avenue Général Leclerc into town and then turn left. | **Hours** The video-monitored parking garage is open around the clock, 365 days a year. | **Tip** There is another underground lot at the Place des Lices.

88__Place des Lices

The easygoing side of St. Tropez

St. Tropez is known for its stars and glamour, its elegant yachts, and its beautiful women. What in the past was a sleepy coastal village, has for decades now been the most popular meeting spot for high society on the French Riviera. Hotels and cafes happily demand a premium based on the city's reputation. But there is still the other St. Tropez, the one that belongs to the locals.

One very special place to experience the town's quiet, serene side is the Place des Lices. Located just two minutes away from the harbor by foot, it's where *boules* players meet in the shade of the sycamore trees. The sandy square is a fixed point of reference for all those from the South of France who want to indulge in their favorite sport, and even in winter the clacking of *boules* can be heard. If you're interested, you can join the spectators on one of the nearby benches to follow the illustrious bustle.

The writer and film director Marcel Pagnol boasted that *boules* – also known as *petanque* – was "the best game man has ever invented." The rules are the simplest in the world: the game is played with two teams of two or three people, each having three balls. The goal is to throw the heavy iron balls, which weigh just under two pounds apiece, as close as possible to the *cochonnet* (literally "piglet"), a small wooden ball tossed about 20 to 30 feet away. The team that reaches 13 points first wins the game. Often a ruler or yardstick will be introduced in order to determine the exact distance between the balls.

And after they've spent a decent amount of time on the *boules* court – a half day at least – competitors gather afterward for a pastis or a glass of wine in the Café des Arts situated on the corner of the Place des Lices. Regular players even have their own dedicated cupboards for their utensils!

Address Place des Lices, 83990 St. Tropez | **Getting there** Located in the town center; follow the signs to the eponymous underground garage. | **Tip** On Tuesday and Saturday mornings, no *boules* is played on the Place des Lices, as a colorful Provençal market is held, where you'll find a wide range of vegetables, fruit, flowers, meat, sausage, cheese, and freshly caught fish.

89 __ Rondini's "Sandales Tropeziennes"

A must-have for shoe lovers

St. Tropez is technically not the center of the fashion universe, but the former fishing village has certainly been known to set a few trends. One such example is the Plage de Pampelonne in St. Tropez: the first beach where it was socially acceptable to go topless.

Another classic fashion fad St. Tropez is known for are the Sandales Tropeziennes of Rondini, chic strappy sandals worn by the likes of Kate Moss, Carla Bruni, and Michelle Obama throughout the summer.

This famous brand was founded in 1927 by Italian immigrant Dominique Rondini. At the time, only a single style was offered – a sandal was still just a sandal. But then along came Brigitte Bardot, who ran through town alongside Alain Delon in a strappy pair. And from that moment forward, every woman wanted to have these simple but durable shoes, and Rondini was barely able to keep up with production.

Rondini's sandals are the result of solid handmade craftsmanship. To this day, the shoes are produced in workshops located in the back of the shop. They can only be purchased in St. Tropez, or ordered by mail. The style selection was greatly expanded quite some time ago. In the store there are sandals in many colors, styles, and various types of leather. Even leather flip-flops (*sahariennes*) are produced. They also now make sandals for men and children, although women are certainly still the focus of the brand.

You should expect to pay at least €100 per pair, but behind each sandal there are hours of work and exactly 46 procedural steps. In the end, Alain Rondini, who is the third generation now to run the business, puts the finishing touches on the sandals by rubbing them with natural leather fat.

Address 18 Rue Georges Clémenceau, 83990 St. Tropez, www.rondini.fr | **Getting there** Rue Georges Clémenceau is a small alley between the Old Port and the Place des Lices. | **Hours** Tue – Sat 9:30am – 6:30pm | **Tip** With K. Jacques, located at 28 Rue Seillon, there is a second sandal manufacturer in St. Tropez (daily 10am – 1pm and 3 – 7pm, www.kjacques.fr).

90__ The Vice Admiral
The terror of the seas

Somehow, Pierre-André de Suffren is a bit lost in the harbor of St. Tropez. Among the illustrious goings-on, his memorial seems strangely out of place. Those sitting at the café tables hardly pay him any attention, because their gaze is instead directed toward the huge yachts in the harbor. "See and be seen," is the motto in St. Tropez – except no one seems to see Vice Admiral Suffren.

So, do you really need to know about this nobleman, born in 1729 in a Provençal castle? The answer is a resounding yes: Pierre-André de Suffren was the third son of the Marquis de St. Tropez and one of the most important French seamen of all time. Suffren joined the navy early in his life, where he made quite a career for himself. During the American Revolution he fired at a British squadron standing in the port at Newport, setting it on fire and gaining a fearsome reputation among the British as the "terror of the seas." Later he was made a commander and a member of the Order of Malta with the title *Bailli de Suffren*. With a squadron of five liners and two frigates, he was sent to the Indian Ocean, where he assisted the Dutch in the battle for colonies in Africa and Asia. Several times he successfully responded to the vessels of the English fleet with equal fire and conquered Trincomalee in Sri Lanka. To thank Suffren, after the Treaty of Paris the French king appointed him vice admiral.

Military historians describe Suffern as the best French naval commander of the 18th century. In his honor, seven ships of the French navy have been christened with his name. But that's not all: on the initiative of Napoleon III, a bronze statue was built for Suffren in 1866 at the pier, which befittingly was cast from the metal of captured cannons. Since then, the vice admiral has looked out over the harbor of St. Tropez and the sea.

Address Quay Suffren, 83990 St. Tropez | **Getting there** Located directly at the Old Port; leave the car at Parking du Port. | **Tip** There is a hotel on the St. Tropez Peninsula named after the vice admiral on the Avenue des Américains. The Hotel de Bailli de Suffren is a luxurious accommodation offering a pool and a gourmet restaurant, both certainly more comfortable than the admiral ever had on his flagship (Tel 0033/(0)498044700, www.lebaillidesuffren.com).

91_ The Bohemian Village
Baby slings, dreadlocks, and organic apple cakes

Saorge is a typical *village perché* (see p.206), clinging to the mountain like an eagle's nest high above the Roya Valley. Due to its hillside location, its houses, with their purple slate roofs, are stacked several floors high. Dark, narrow alleys wind between them, interconnected by slim flights of stairs.

For centuries, Saorge controlled access to the valley floor and thereby controlled the trade route to Cuneo, in nearby Piedmont. It was not until 1794 that the town surrendered to the Republican troops of General Masséna. Saorge not only lost its strategic importance then, but also large parts of its population, in the context of rural-urban migration.

Since the 1960s, Saorge has become increasingly popular with those looking to leave the rat race behind, and many have settled in the vacant houses and small farms of the village. It made sense for the scandalous French author, Michel Houellebecq, to set a chapter of his novel *The Elementary Particles* in Saorge, where the hippie mother of the protagonist, Bruno, has withdrawn to pass her final days. The village still has a lively alternative scene, which is also reflected in the town's politics: in no other constituency in the département have the Greens garnered more votes than in Saorge.

Here it is common to see men with long beards and dreadlocks and mothers who carry their babies through the village in colorful cloth slings. The social and cultural center of town is La Petite Épicerie, a wonderful mom-and-pop shop and café. There they sell local eggs, olives, and cheese, as well as home-baked organic apple cakes, and offer a daily changing lunch menu. The community message board of the Épicerie is still the most used form of information exchange in the village – even in the age of the Internet.

Address 06540 Saorge | **Getting there** Saorge is located about 19 miles north of Menton on the D 6204, which continues on to Cuneo, in Italy. | **Hours** La Petite Épicerie is open daily | **Tip** The Baroque former Franciscan monastery on the outskirts of town has a pretty frescoed cloister.

92 __ Chatwin's Castle
The last refuge of the restless nomad

To avoid misunderstandings, let's start straightaway with a clari-
fication: Bruce Chatwin was never the actual owner of the Château
of Seillans, but the castle served as the last refuge for the restless
nomad, who, as the author of the cult favorites *The Songlines* and *In
Patagonia*, is still counted among the most well-known travel writers
in the world.

The Château is perched atop a hill overlooking the old town of
Seillans. The oldest parts of the castle date back to the 11th century,
but through the years it has been rebuilt and expanded several times.
Over the course of the centuries, there has been a lively change
of ownership, which even included, at one point, the Comtesse
de Savigny. Finally, the Château was bought by the author Shirley
Conran. Chatwin – who was not only close friends with the ex-wife
of designer Sir Terence Conran, but also at times the lover of her
son Jasper – used the Château at Shirley's invitation, beginning in
December 1986, as his permanent residence abroad. On the beautiful terrace overlooking the hills of Provence, Chatwin penned his
novel *Utz*, but by then things were already starting to look bad for
the author's health.

Although the course of the disease was indisputable, Bruce
Chatwin, who never publicly came out of the closet, denied vehe-
mently that he was suffering from AIDS. Instead, he offered theories
of an unexplainable fever and a rare fungus that had attacked his
internal organs. He continued to travel the world as best he could,
but as his condition worsened, Chatwin moved back to Seillans late
in the autumn of 1988, where he hoped in vain for improvement. At
the end, he had to rely on a voice recorder, because he no longer had
the strength to write. He was hospitalized on January 16, 1989, in
Nice, where he died two days later.

Address 83440 Seillans | **Getting there** Seillans is located 12.5 miles northeast of Draguignan on the D 19 between Fayence and Bargemon. | **Tip** At the steps to the castle is a stirring and mysterious bronze sculpture called *Dragon de Seillans* by the artist Yvan Ivanoff.

93___Hôtel des Deux Rocs

A country hotel straight out of a picture book

If you are in search of *the* perfect country hotel, you should definitely put Seillans on your travel itinerary, because the Deux Rocs comes pretty close to the ideal.

Situated at the top of the village next to the castle, this mansion from the 17th century has been transformed into a seductive inn enveloped in a fine patina. The wooden floors creak, and the stone stairs are slightly beveled. There are a dozen lovingly furnished guest rooms spread out over two floors, each decorated according to a different design motif. The individualized interiors include fabric-covered walls, antique furniture, and framed portraits, and even the seemingly antiquated bathrooms, with their claw-footed bathtubs, leave no comforts behind. Fortunately for everyone, the price is not out of the range of an average three-star hotel.

Named after the famous *Deux Rocs*, a striking two-headed rock formation, the hotel also exudes charm and warmth, because Julie and Nicolas Malzac, who met at hotel school, are lovable hosts who strive to create a familiar and inviting atmosphere for their guests. In the attached restaurant, you will be treated to Provençal cuisine of the highest level, interpreted both traditionally and with a more modern twist.

Every bit as lovely as the hotel itself, the cobblestone terrace in front is simply an outdoor extension of the building. From the handful of tables and chairs arranged around the stone fountain, which efficiently cools the white wine, guests have a magnificent view of the surrounding hills, and two majestic sycamore trees provide more than enough shade in the summer heat. In nice weather, the hotel serves breakfast, including homemade jams, outside. When the rain starts, guests meet in the salon by the cozy fireplace.

Address 1 Place Font d'Amont, 83440 Seillans, Tel 0033/(0)494768732, www.hoteldeuxrocs.com | **Getting there** Seillans is located 12.5 miles northeast of Draguignan on the D 19 between Fayence and Bargemon. The hotel is on the upper edge of the village next to the castle. | **Tip** The restaurant is open to the public, not just hotel guests. The neighboring village of Bargemon is also well worth a visit.

94__Le Génie de la Bastille
Max Ernst's surrealist totem pole

On the boules court in Seillans the balls clack together, players work together toward their goal with zeal, and barely a soul pays any attention to *Le Génie de la Bastille*, the bronze statue that has stood at the sandy edge of the court since 1994, the work of the great surrealist artist Max Ernst, who, in 1964, chose dreamy Seillans for his retirement.

Together with his last wife, Dorothea Tanning, Ernst initially lived and worked near the castle in a house named *La Dolce Vita*. In 1970, the couple picked up and moved into a villa built above the village with a studio and swimming pool shaped like a keyhole, the *Mas de Saint Roch*. Today, an iron entry gate designed by Max Ernst with a stylized head recalls the great surrealist. After the artist's death in 1976, Dorothea Tanning left tranquil Seillans to return to New York. When she visited her Provençal home in 1994, she gifted *Le Génie de la Bastille* to the community, and the piece can now be admired at the edge of the boules court. The location of the stele was not chosen at random; Max Ernst had happily spent hours playing boules with the locals on the court at the town's entrance.

The roughly 10-foot-high column, which is topped by a birdlike hybrid with a beaked nose, stubby wings, and round eyes, was created while Ernst was in exile in America. He lived in Sedona, Arizona, at the time, where the totem poles of the Native Americans provided inspiration for the work he originally erected next to his house. At the same time, the artist, who was never shy when it came to creating a bit of mischief, parodied the monumental freedom column on the Place de la Bastille in Paris with the name of the sculpture. Worldwide, twelve castings have been created from the original piece, and one of them now shines in the sun in the South of France.

Address Place de la République, 83440 Seillans | **Getting there** Seillans is located 12.5 miles northeast of Draguignan on the D 19 between Fayence and Bargemon. The boules court is located on the western edge of town. Parking is available. | **Tip** Lithographs by Max Ernst and Dorothea Tanning are on display in the Musée Waldberg (Apr–Sep, Tue–Fri 10am–12:30pm and 2–5:30pm, Sat 2–5:30pm).

95_ The Toll Bridge

Salt + bridge = wealth

Sospel is one of the largest towns in the French Maritime Alps with more than 3,000 residents, but it nonetheless has a pretty sleepy vibe. It is hard to imagine that in the Middle Ages more than three times as many people lived here. At that time, Sospel was the second-largest city in the whole county of Nice. Sospel particularly benefited during this period from its location in the wide valley carved by the small river Bévéra, since several important trade routes intersected here, including the Route du Sel.

The town owes its wealth and good fortune to this "road of salt." Anyone looking to cross the Bévéra in Sospel was forced to pay a toll. A bridge that included a customs house was built spanning the river, and its striking silhouette has been the symbol of the community for ages. It is no longer visible in its original state, however, because it was badly damaged during the heavy bombardments in October 1944, during World War II. A difficult reconstruction was undertaken and completed in 1953.

The stone bridge was also important to the local community because Sospel is a town in two pieces: on the right bank of the river is the charming medieval town center and the Cathédrale Saint-Michel, while on the left is the neighborhood of Saint-Nicolas, whose center is paved with river stones. The Place Saint-Nicolas also sits on the left bank, lined by arcades reminiscent of the town's Italian past as Sospello.

The Cathédrale houses an altarpiece by François Brea, an artist who worked in the 16th century in the county of Nice and Liguria just as his more famous uncle, Louis Bréa, did. In the center of the triptych is the *Virgin of the Immaculate Conception*, framed by two saints, a motif that the artist depicted fondly in the time of the Counter-Reformation.

Address 06380 Sospel | **Getting there** Sospel lies along the D 2204 halfway between Nice and Breil-sur-Roya. The bridge is located in the town center spanning the two halves of the city. | **Tip** In the immediate vicinity of Sospel is Fort Saint-Roche, which was part of the Maginot Line (Apr–Oct, Sat and Sun 2–6pm, in high season Tue–Sun 2–5pm).

96__ The Museum of Wonders
Prehistoric graffiti art

Those who drive along the road through the small town of Tende without doing their research beforehand are likely to wonder about the conspicuous white-tiled pillars sporting mysterious symbols in front of the slightly recessed Musée des Merveilles building. A permanent exhibition of graffiti art in the French Maritime Alps? Not exactly. These are, in fact, representations of prehistoric rock carvings found on the slopes of nearby Mont Bégo.

The Vallée des Merveilles ("Valley of Wonders"), perched high in the mountains and spilling over into the adjacent valleys, is regarded as one of Europe's largest open-air museums of prehistory. The indigenous peoples of Liguria began to carve drawings in the dark rock more than 4,000 years ago. The majority of the more than 35,000 engravings, which were made at an altitude between 6,890 and 8,530 feet, date from the years 1800 to 1500 BC, during the Bronze Age.

Initially it was thought that the characters were indecipherable, but we now know that these early mountain dwellers scratched representations of real-life objects into the rock. Researchers have concluded that more than half the drawings can be classified into four general categories: weapons and tools, geometric figures, human figures, and cattle horns. It remains a mystery, however, whether the rock carvings were done for ritualistic or other reasons.

In the Musée des Merveilles, casts of the most impressive rock carvings are displayed next to other archaeological finds (tools, vessels, etc.). The permanent exhibition also provides insights into natural history as well as regional folk art, whereby, through dioramas, graphical representations, and audiovisual and multi-media materials, the living conditions of ancient times are vividly represented.

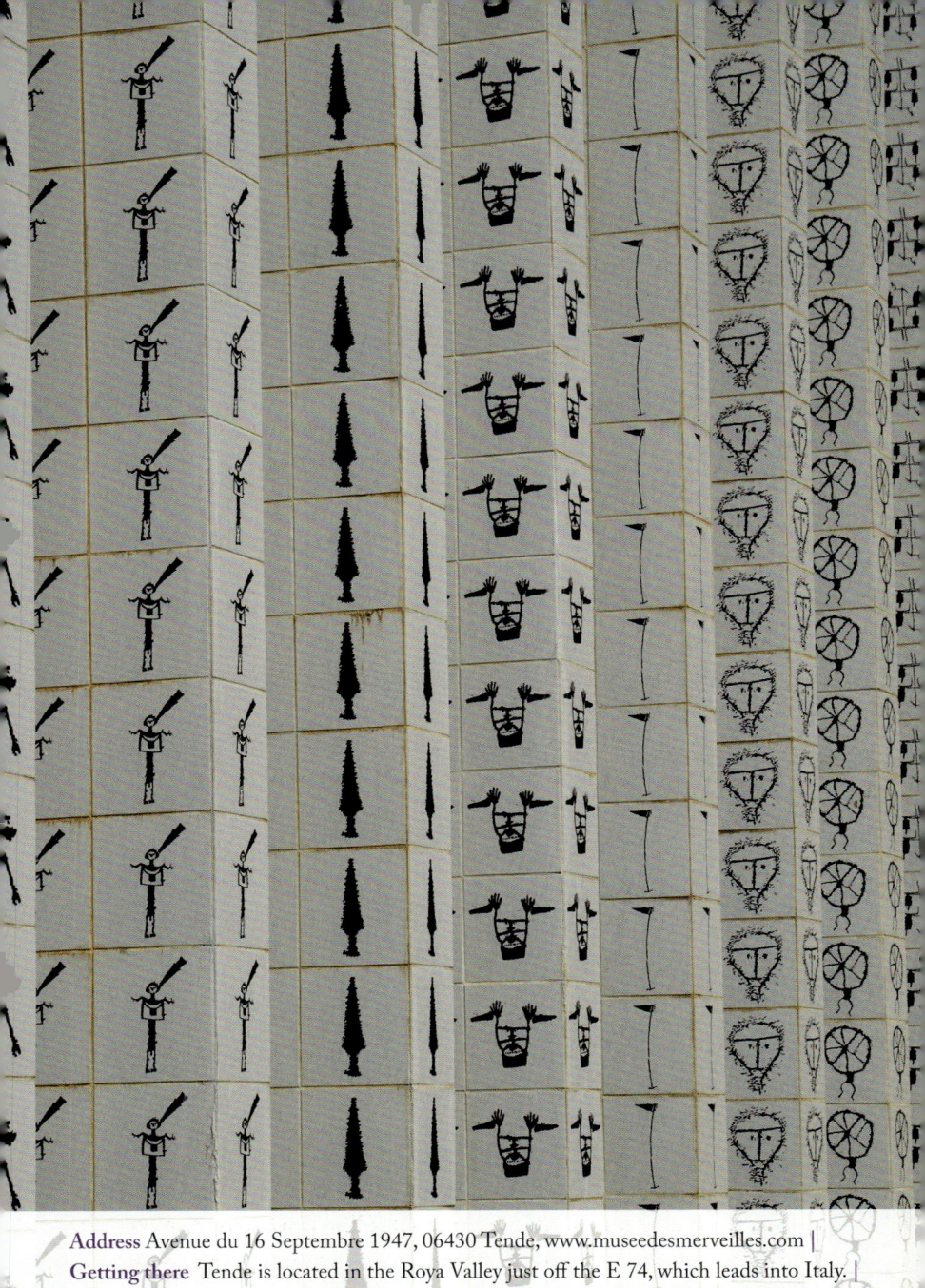

Address Avenue du 16 Septembre 1947, 06430 Tende, www.museedesmerveilles.com |
Getting there Tende is located in the Roya Valley just off the E 74, which leads into Italy. |
Hours May–Oct 15, Mon, Wed–Sun 10am–6:30pm (also Tue in July and Aug); in winter,
Mon, Wed–Sun 10am–5pm; in both mid-Mar and mid-Nov the museum closes for two
weeks | **Tip** During the summer, it's about a three-hour hike up from Castérino to the
petroglyphs of the Vallée des Merveilles.

97__Tunnel du Col de Tende

Two miles straight through the mountain

For those traveling to the French Riviera from the north through Turin and the Po Valley, the Col de Tende serves as the monumental gateway to France. The border between France and Italy runs right through the peak of the 6,138-foot-high mountain pass. For centuries, all goods – especially much-coveted salt – that were destined for the Italian region of Piedmont had to be transported over narrow mule tracks up to the Col de Tende.

It is almost impossible to imagine how difficult it must have been, negotiating the Alpine mountain pass during that time. On his visit to the region in 1765, the Scottish physician and writer Tobias Smollett described himself as "speechless in the face of this famous and dangerous mountain."

There must have been some traders even then who thought that it would be easier and faster to go through the mountain rather than over it, but the technology for such an undertaking was still quite a way off. It wasn't until the second half of the 19th century that plans for the impressive road tunnel were finalized. It was finally completed in 1882, after more than nine years of construction work. With a length of nearly two miles, it was not only the longest road tunnel in the world when it opened, but also the first under an Alpine pass.

Although 8,000 vehicles pass through the Tunnel du Col de Tende daily in the summer, it is considered one of the most dangerous road tunnels in Europe because it is only 20 feet wide. There is only one lane for traffic, so long lines of cars often form at the traffic lights. To remedy this unacceptable condition, construction has begun on a second tunnel, which is expected to open in 2020. In the course of the work, the old tunnel will also be brought up to the latest standards in safety engineering.

Address 06430 Tende | **Getting there** The Tende tunnel is located at the northern end of the RN 204, which runs from Breil-sur-Roya to Cuneo. | **Tip** It is still a great drive around the 46 hairpin turns of the actual pass. The highest 16 turns are not paved, however, so the gravel road is best managed with an all-terrain vehicle or a mountain bike.

98__ The Rust-Brown Spaceship

The Palais Bulles by Antti Lovag

Don't worry: no extraterrestrials have crash-landed in Théoule-sur-Mer. And those are not space capsules floating on the hill overlooking the sea. Rather, what you see is the Palais Bulles ("Palace of Bubbles"), a futuristic estate built between 1975 and 1991 by French-Hungarian architect Antti Lovag for industrialist Pierre Bernard. Locals refer to the extravagant home, acquired in 1992 by fashion magnate Pierre Cardin, both lovingly and sarcastically as a "rust-brown spaceship."

Lovag, who passed away in 2014, was considered a true visionary of modern architecture when it came to his bubble houses. His goal was to create biomorphic habitats whose rounded, cornerless forms, inspired by caves and igloos, would meet basic human needs for security. Lovag put high demands on his clients, though, since he refused to give cost estimates or draw up plans for his projects. In carrying them out, he used a spiderweb of steel, which he then coated with a mixture of plastic and concrete. The reddish-brown exterior coat applied was meant to recall the colors of the Esterel Mountains.

The Palais Bulles was not originally designed to be used for residential purposes, but rather as a communication center. A total of 25 "bubbles" spread over four levels cover an area of nearly 13,000 square feet. A maze of interlocking halls and pathways connects the various spaces: offices, a cinema, a library, and ten suites with porthole-like windows designed to allow maximum exposure to the excellent views of the Mediterranean landscape. The kitchen was mounted on rails so as to rotate into the open. The complex is surrounded by a lush garden with two swimming pools and a 500-seat amphitheater.

Address Boulevard de l'Esterel, 06590 Théoule-sur-Mer, www.palaisbulles.com | **Getting there** Théoule-sur-Mer is about three miles southwest of Cannes, on the coastal road (D 6098). | **Tip** About 1.25 miles northeast there is a great day hike to the Pointe de l'Aiguille, a prominent rock projecting into the sea with an adjacent beach.

99___ The Preserved Village
Stacked up to the heavens

It would take only the addition of a few colorful prayer flags fluttering in the wind here to make you think that you were high up on a Tibetan plateau. The ocher-colored houses of Touët-sur-Var pile up on a steep rock face along the slope. It is a scene that is picturesque in the truest sense of the word.

There is no question: Touët-sur-Var is one of the most beautiful villages in the entire Département Alpes-Maritimes. Due to its particular location, the village could not be expanded out any further, so its ancient appearance has been preserved. A newer settlement was established on the more accessible valley floor, where the station for the Train des Pignes has been located since 1888. You can reach the old town in about 10 minutes via a panoramic trail.

For protection against enemies, the houses were built atop one another so that their outer walls formed a sort of small fortification, which, in an emergency, also allowed residents to easily defend themselves. On the inside, the partially vaulted streets are scrambled like a maze, so that enemy attackers would lose their orientation. Touët is therefore considered a classic example of a so-called *village perché*.

In the village itself, you will be overcome by the colorful scene: more than 70 doors have been painted by artists as part of an ongoing project, and the designs are so variegated and fanciful that the few simply depicting the sea seem banal and out of place.

Most of the houses have a south-facing open loft called a *soleilloir*, which was traditionally used for drying figs. The town's Romanesque church even boasts a small curiosity: it was built on a mountain stream, which you can still see and hear roaring through a sort of covered gully under the center aisle.

While here, don't miss out on the people-watching in the village's attractive main square.

Address 06710 Touët-sur-Var | **Getting there** Touët-sur-Var is about 35 miles from Nice in the valley of the Var, right on the D 6202. | **Tip** You'll get a wonderful view of the Var Valley on a hike up to the Crête de la Chabasse.

100__Sentier des Douaniers

Along the historic trails of the coast

One of the finest ways to explore the coast of the Département Var is to hike along the coastal path, called the Sentier des Douaniers. We can thank none other than Napoleon for this unique trail. During the time of his reign, he wanted, on the one hand, to protect the French coast from invasion, and, on the other hand, for the continental blockade against England to prevail and prevent not only weapons, but also salt, tobacco, and other goods from being smuggled into the country. Thanks to his imperial decree, any owner of a coastal landholding had to see to it that a three-meter-wide path could be laid along the water. Armed customs officers then patrolled the coast, which until then had been mostly inaccessible, in order to curb the activities of smugglers.

Napoleon and the continental blockade are part of the past, but the coastal path remains. Over time, the path became overgrown in many places, and in some stretches it was also overbuilt or obstructed by walls. Only in 1976 did the path return to the forefront of people's minds, and it was once again made accessible – at least as much as possible.

A scenically attractive portion of the "path of the toll collectors" extends east from Toulon and leads over to Hyères. It begins in the neighborhood of Mourillon, located at the harbor, where the officers and captains of merchant and naval ships primarily lived. The path starts out as a promenade that passes three artificially created swimming bays and the Rade des Vignettes. But it soon opens into a true hiking trail, running extremely close to the sea and leading up to Cap Brun. It then continues on to Anse de Méjan, a crescent-shaped bay with good swimming opportunities, where you can also admire some of the popular fishing huts used in the summertime, known as *cabanons*.

Address 83000 Toulon | **Getting there** Toulon is in the western part of the French Riviera and can be reached quickly and easily on several highways. The path starts at the Littoral Frédéric Mistral, about a half mile southeast of the harbor. | **Tip** Toulon isn't the only place you can follow in the footsteps of the customs officers. There are also trails between Six-Fours and La Seyne-sur-Mer, and between L'Argentère and Fort Brégançon.

101__ The Butterfly and the Beetle

Memories of Bernard Buffet

Tourtour clings precariously to a mountainside as if it were on display for all to see. Even the Celts appreciated this about the spot: the name Tourtour is derived from *tur*, the Celtic term for an easily visible geographical location. And that visibility is indeed impressive: in good weather, the view from Tourtour extends from the Gulf of Saint-Raphaël to the Montagne Sainte-Victoire. An incredibly beautiful market square, authentic stone houses, and the remains of a medieval city fortification complete the picturesque scenery.

In other words, Tourtour is the ideal home for visually stimulated people and artists such as Bernard Buffet, who, in 1986, discovered the village by chance. Buffet set up a studio for himself in the northeast part of Tourtour at the pretty country estate of Domaine de la Baume, where he lived and worked with his wife, Annabel, until his death.

Buffet is counted among the most renowned French painters of the twentieth century, and his works belong to the collections of many major museums, including London's Tate Gallery and the Musée National d'Art Moderne in Paris. His paintings, generally attributed to existentialism, commanded extremely high prices at art auctions for quite some time, but by the late 1960s they began to be considered overvalued and disappeared into the vaults. When he could no longer paint due to his progressive Parkinson's disease, he took his own life in his home on October 4, 1999.

After Buffet's death his widow donated two huge bronze sculptures to the community, which he had created in his home in Tourtour. The modern representations of a butterfly and a beetle have been placed in a square near the town hall.

Address Route d'Aups, 83690 Tourtour | **Getting there** Tourtour is located 12.5 miles west of Draguignan on the D 51. | **Tip** Very attractive rooms are now rented in the Domaine de la Baume as *chambres d'hôtes* (Tel 0033/(0)457747474, www.domaine-delabaume.com).

102—The Pilgrimage Chapel
A sanctuary on high

There are hardly any pilgrimage chapels built in the depths of a ravine. It was usually a small hilltop or mountain peak that was crowned by such a house of worship, so that the location in itself would free the faithful from the burden of worldly possessions and the difficulty of our earthly existence. In addition, the physical exertion of the arduous pilgrimage provides for a fully immersive experience.

The pilgrimage site of Sanctuaire de la Madone d'Utelle was founded by Spanish seafarers in the middle of the 9th century. After they were led safely to shore by a bright star during a heavy storm, they fulfilled their promise to build and dedicate a chapel to the mother of God. Since then, the faithful have flocked to the 3,850-foot-high sanctuary. But as the original chapel was destroyed during the French Revolution, today's chapel dates back only to the year 1806. In particular, excitement reigns over the site every year on Easter Monday (Whit Monday), on August 15, and on September 8. On these days, mass is held outdoors under the open sky, and those making the pilgrimage are rewarded with a magnificent panoramic view: to the summit chain of the Maritime Alps with Mont Mounier, Cime de Argentera, and Mont Bégo in the north; to Cap d'Antibes and the Lérins Islands in the south.

There is fortunately also a 3.7-mile-long access road winding up from Utelle to the plateau where the pilgrimage chapel stands. Once at the top, a detailed orientation board informs visitors about the surrounding peaks.

The Hôtellerie du Sanctuaire directly adjacent to the chapel offers guests drinks and delicious food on its garden terrace. In addition to a couple of inexpensive beds for overnight stays, there is also a small shop selling local products and souvenirs.

Address 06450 Utelle, www.madonedutelle.com | **Getting there** From the valley of the Vésubie, the D 32 winds up to Utelle. At the end it is a further 3.7 miles to the chapel. | **Hours** Daily 9am–6pm | **Tip** The village of Utelle, located below the chapel, also has a pretty church, Saint-Véran, with a richly decorated door depicting scenes from the life of the eponymous saint.

103_ The Grave of Actor Jean Marais

Beautiful and beastly

Every tomb inherently conveys a message about its inhabitant to posterity. Some find their final resting place under a plainly adorned grave slab or simply have their ashes scattered in the sea; others opt for more opulence, be it a tall headstone or burial in a fancy mausoleum. The grave of Jean Marais is a final homage to one of his best-known films: *La Belle et la Bête*, or *Beauty and the Beast*, in which Marais excelled in his dual role as both the beast and the handsome prince.

Jean Marais spent the majority of his life happily living on the French Riviera. He began his time here spending summers in Villefranche-sur-Mer and on the Cap Ferrat, and later lived permanently in Cabris. In this small village located close to Grasse, he commissioned the construction of a villa that he designed himself and lived in for 20 years, until his death on November 8, 1998. During this period, he often came to Vallauris, where he not only worked on pottery and opened an art gallery, but also was integral in establishing a theater festival. The city's leaders appointed him an honorary citizen of their community due to his extensive cultural engagement.

Based on his personal request, Jean Marais was buried in the Vieux Cimetière ("old cemetery"), in Vallauris. Situated about 500 feet from the entrance, the self-designed grave of the eccentric actor is hard to miss. Marais, who shot half a dozen films together with Jean Cocteau, was inspired by the poetic romance of *La Belle et la Bête*, first screened in 1946 at the Cannes film festival. The masks and accessories from the film provide his grave with a distinct aura of fantasy, and the marble headstone is crowned by a sphinx with deer antlers.

Address Montée Sainte-Anne, 06220 Vallauris | **Getting there** Vallauris is located between Cannes and Antibes. The small town is reached from Golfe Juan via the D 135; the Montée Sainte-Anne lies on a side street. | **Hours** May–Oct, daily 7:30am–7pm; Nov–Apr, daily 7:30am–5pm | **Tip** A permanent exhibition of the actor's photography and pottery is on display in the Espace Jean Marais at 3 Avenue des Martyrs de la Résistance (July and Aug, daily 10am–1pm and 3–7pm, otherwise Tue–Sat 10am–12:30pm and 2–5:30pm).

104_ Homme au Mouton
A gift to the city

The French Riviera was the adopted home of Pablo Picasso, in part because the Mediterranean climate and landscape reminded him of the Spain of his childhood. After the end of the World War II, he lived first in a small house in Golfe-Juan with Françoise Gilot, then kept a studio in the Château of Antibes; next he moved for a time to Vallauris, after which he lived in Cannes, and finally settled in Mougins, where he chose to spend his retirement. Fortunately, Picasso's art on the Côte d'Azur is found not only in museums, but also in a public square in Vallauris.

Vallauris is a small town whose local tradition of pottery dates back to the late Middle Ages. Picasso became fascinated by the art of pottery when he made the acquaintance of Georges and Suzanne Ramié in August 1946, and they invited him to their ceramics workshop in Vallauris. After his initial skepticism, Picasso came to enjoy working with the unfamiliar material, and he continued to do so for nearly two years in their studio. Many of the pieces he created during this time can be admired today at the Picasso Museum in Antibes.

A gift from the artist provided most of the museum's collection. Picasso was always very generous in this regard. He even reciprocated the thanks he received from the city's leaders. In 1950, when the municipality named him an honorary citizen and hosted a gala in his honor, Picasso gave the city the bronze cast of a plaster sculpture, *Homme au Mouton* (Man with Sheep), which he had made in 1943 in Paris as a sign of hope and peace. The sculpture, a touching and realistic representation, still stands today in the middle of the market square in the heart of Vallauris. Ironically, the sculpture makes an interesting contrast to the menacing and pompous War Memorial, which stands opposite it on the other side of the square.

Address Place Isnard, 06220 Vallauris | **Getting there** Vallauris is located between Cannes and Antibes. You can reach the small city via the D 135 from Golfe Juan. The Place Isnard lies in the upper part of the old town. | **Tip** Nearby on the Place de la Libération, there is a Romanesque chapel with Picasso's famous mural *La Guerre et la Paix* (War and Peace). It has been declared a National Museum (Mon, Wed–Sun, and holidays 10am–12:15pm and 2–5pm; July and Aug, 10am–7pm, www.musee-picasso-vallauris.fr).

Pablo Picasso
L'homme au mouton
Bronze offert par le MAÎTRE en 1949
A la ville de Vallauris Golfe-Juan

105_ The Caves

An unusual castle in the rocks

Villecroze was inhabited as far back as prehistoric times: the village's name (*ville creusée* in modern French) still recalls how the first houses were laboriously dug into the soft tufa rock. In late antiquity, the Romans established a small settlement but its residents fell victim to a Saracen attack. Later, a Benedictine monastery was built here, which was taken over by the Knights Templar, who were in turn replaced by the Maltese. The cross-shaped plan of the village, with houses integrated into the city walls, bears witness to its defensive character.

At first glance, Villecroze is a typical village of the Haut-Var region: narrow streets, a few arcades and cafes, and a village square filled with sycamores. It's the perfect place to leisurely spend a few quiet days. But those who travel a few minutes north will find themselves, unexpectedly, in the middle of a gorgeous park. With its palm trees, exotic plants, and a wide waterfall that pours down spectacularly over a cliff from a height of nearly 115 feet, the scenery is downright heavenly. It is only upon close inspection that you'll discover next to the waterfall a pair of windows and walls that appear like honeycombs built into the rocks.

The windows belong to an unusual 16th-century castle in front of the caves, built by a nobleman named Nicolas d'Albertas because he was afraid of marauding bands during the religious wars. The fortress consists of several spaces of varying sizes, some with ceilings as high as 23 feet.

Some of the castle's interior walls are damp and gleam mysteriously in the light. The rock chambers are connected through stairs and narrow gaps, and in the rear portion, the roughly 700,000-year-old caves are also fascinating thanks to their stalactites and an underground lake.

Address 83690 Villecroze | **Getting there** Villecroze is 12.5 miles west of Draguignan on the D 557. The park is located on the northern edge of the village. | **Hours** July – Aug, daily 10am – 1pm and 3 – 6:30pm; Sep – Jun, Mon, Fri, Sat and Sun 2 – 6pm | **Tip** The village comes alive on Thursday mornings with a colorful Provençal market.

106_ Chapelle Saint-Pierre
To each painter his chapel

Jean Cocteau (1895–1963), who for decades spent his summers in Villefranche-sur-Mer (see p.226), probably walked past the small Romanesque harbor chapel innumerable times without paying it any attention. The crumbling church, which is dedicated to Saint Peter, the patron saint of fishermen, was at that time used only to store fishing nets and equipment. Religious services had long since ceased to be held there.

But after Matisse created the wall decorations and the glass windows of the Chapelle du Rosier in Vence, and Picasso had immortalized himself in Vallauris with the wall fresco *War and Peace*, Cocteau began brooding and finally remembered the harbor chapel standing vacant. How could an artist not have his own church, after all?

Cocteau went to the city council in 1956 and managed to convince the mayor to entrust the renovation of the church to him. Cocteau worked in the small nave for five months to decorate it with scenes from the life of Saint Peter. He fancifully painted his own interpretation of the apostle's life in soft pastel colors on the wall: a poetic tribute with fishing and gypsy motifs, surrounded by angels and apostles, whose eyes are vaguely reminiscent of fish eyes. When questioned about his own faith, Cocteau replied coquettishly: "I believe in the God who believes in my chapel...."

Pablo Picasso, who was among the first to view the frescoes, harbored certain doubts about the motives of the painting poet: "Jean is so eager to talk about it, that it would seem he is imagining painting the Saint Lazare train station next." And when the actor Noël Coward visited the chapel with Greta Garbo, he was surprised to note that all the apostles looked suspiciously like Cocteau's good friend, Jean Marais.

Address Quai Amiral Courbet, 06230 Villefranche-sur-Mer | **Getting there** A few miles east of Nice, right on the coastal road (M 6098). A spur road leads down to the harbor. | **Hours** Easter–Oct, Tue–Sun 10am–12pm and 3–7pm | **Tip** Jean Cocteau was often a guest at La Mère Germaine, the harborside restaurant located on the Quai de l'Amiral Courbet. It is known for its delicious seafood (Tel 0033/(0)493017139, www.meregermaine.com).

107 _ Citadelle Saint-Elme

Art in place of guns

Villefranche-sur-Mer was originally founded as a free port. For quite a long time, the town was a part of the Duchy of Savoy, and it was built out as a bulwark against its neighbor, France. In order to protect the harbor, an imposing citadel was built, whose powerful cannons ruled over the entire bay of Villefranche. With its jagged ramparts, deep trenches, and meter-thick walls that extend all the way down to the sea, the citadel met the most modern requirements for defensive fortifications of the time.

It took a long time for Villefranche's military tradition to come to an end: it was not until 1962 that the American naval forces – the very deep harbor basin was also suitable for their large warships – finally departed from their base on the French Mediterranean coast. The city then acquired the fortress and not only moved their town hall to the site, but also used the space as an art museum and forum.

Since that time, various art collections have been presented in the buildings that used to house the barracks, which have been repainted in bright yellow and red earth tones. Most impressive is the sculpture collection of local artist Antoniucci Volti, who has worked in bronze, copper, and clay (Fondation Volti). Some of his metaphorical sculptures can be admired in the open spaces of the site. The Musée Goetz-Boumeester – a foundation created by the artistic couple Henri Goetz and Christine Boumeester, who have close ties with Villefranche – also has a small collection of works by Picasso, Miró, Picabia, and Hartung. Anyone interested in historical ceramic figures should visit the Collection Roux.

The military tradition has not been completely forgotten: in a small part of the citadel, the 24th Battalion of the French Alpine Infanterie, who were stationed here from 1876 to 1939, is remembered.

Address Rue de la Citadelle, 06230 Villefranche-sur-Mer | **Getting there** A few miles east of Nice, right on the coastal road (M 6098). A spur road leads down to the harbor. | **Hours** Oct and Dec–May, 10am–12pm and 2–5:30pm; June and Sep, 9am–12pm and 2:30–6pm; July and Aug, 10am–12pm and 2:30–7pm, closed Sunday afternoon, Tuesdays, and in November | **Tip** There is an open-air cinema (Cinéma de Plein Air) in the citadel from mid-June to mid-September every evening at 9:30pm.

108_ The Rue Obscure

A road to the underworld

Villefranche-sur-Mer is a small, lively harbor town with a mighty citadel, which reminds visitors today that for centuries this place served as a Savoy bulwark against France. Along the quay, restaurants display their fresh seafood sitting atop piles of ice, and houses pile up the cliffs behind the waterfront. But as soon as you leave the harbor and stroll over into one of the narrow streets, you'll find yourself in a dark, mysterious world.

Parallel to the port stretches the Rue Obscure, an almost completely overbuilt road, about 425 feet long, which runs along the original medieval city walls. It will take you a moment to adjust your senses, as the light is dimmer here and the air pleasantly cool even in the midst of summer. Originally, the Rue Obscure, which dates from the late 13th century, facilitated the execution of defensive military maneuvers, allowing troops to carry them out without being seen by adversaries from the water. In later years, the alley offered the population protection from the cannon blasts of enemy ships.

Covered by arcades, the alley is like a dark tunnel that absorbs sunlight from above and noise from the sea below. If you walk alone here during the evening hours, your imagination will run wild and can easily conjure up scenes straight out of a horror flick. Jean Cocteau used the mystical atmosphere of the quirky street to shoot scenes for his film *Le Testament d'Orphée*. Later, various excesses would descend upon the place, particularly in the 1970s when the Rolling Stones repeatedly threw wild parties in Villefranche-sur-Mer and, in the opinion of some people, corrupted the youth of the village. The Stones, incidentally, recorded their famous album *Exile on Main St.* in the basement of the Villa Nellcôte in Villefranche, which was being rented by Keith Richards.

Address Rue Obscure, 06230 Villefranche-sur-Mer | **Getting there** A few miles east of Nice, right on the coastal road (M 6098). A spur road leads down to the harbor. | **Tip** Those who crave a bit of sunlight after visiting the dark alley can happily swim at the Plage des Marinières at the eastern end of town.

109__ Welcome Hôtel
High times in the hotel for artists

To avoid creating any false expectations: the wild days are definitely over! Nevertheless, the Welcome Hôtel still draws today on its legendary reputation from the 1920s, when Jean Cocteau and his artist friends let loose here to the fullest extent. The village of Villefranche, built on a slope, was considered *the* meeting place for gay men and women on the French Riviera at the time. Cocteau stayed several summers with his clique in the relatively simple lodgings of the Welcome. Here he put the finishing touches on his film *Orpheus*, and had his fun with the young sailors from the military ships who were moored nearby. "We painted, we wrote, we visited each other from room to room."

Cocteau's favorite guest room was the one in the corner overlooking the harbor. Like an opera box, from here he could watch the bustle unfold below on the jetty. It must have been a wonderful time for him and his friends. As the smell of opium flowed through the halls of the "haunted hotel," the famous model Kiki de Montparnasse clashed with local prostitutes and was arrested at the bar after she hit a police officer who intervened. The photographer Man Ray generously took care of the fine, and Kiki was set free once again.

In the imaginary guest book of the Welcome Hôtel there are also entries for Oscar Wilde, Charles Baudelaire, Isadora Duncan, Albert Einstein, Errol Flynn, and André Gide. Erika and Klaus Mann wrote in a 1931 travel guide stating that among the hotels in Villefranche, the Welcome was "the only one that you should question staying in." And this still applies today: the location of the hotel is fantastic, but everything is just a bit less snazzy than in its heyday. And we must also strongly advise against using opium – even cigarettes must now be smoked out on the balcony!

Address 3 Quai Amiral Courbet, 06230 Villefranche-sur-Mer, Tel 0033/(0)493762762, www.welcomehotel.com | **Getting there** A few miles east of Nice, right on the coastal road (M 6098). A spur road leads down to the harbor. | **Tip** The city's leaders honored Cocteau with a bust in 1989, which they installed opposite the Welcome Hôtel. It quotes the artist: "When I look at Villefranche, I see my youth."

110 Marina Baie des Anges

Artfully stacked vacation dreams

The 1960s were a period of economic growth for much of Europe. Industrialized countries such as Germany and France prospered, wealth increased, and living conditions improved. Workers were given more vacation time, and a greater number of people could afford a vacation or even a second home somewhere in the warmer south.

Because land was expensive and sparse not only in Paris but also on the Riviera, people began to build vertically. The most spectacular construction project during those years was a vacation resort called the Marina Baie des Anges, which was built in 1968 at the end of the Bay of Angels on a previously barren stretch of land between the sea and the railway line. The architect André Minangoy designed the modern resort with shops, doctors' offices, and a marina with a capacity for 530 yachts.

Marina Baie des Anges consists of four giant, curving building complexes. Each resembles an enormous white sail, with its balconies cascading down on top of one another like a waterfall. In each of the buildings – christened with the flowery names l'Amiral, le Baronnet, le Commodore, and le Ducal – there are about 330 apartments that extend from north to south to provide a view of the sea. For a "nominal" fee, mooring for your boat is included. In other words, it is the ideal place for wealthy pensioners who want to spend the twilight of their lives in a high-rise with sunshine guaranteed.

The construction project was highly controversial when completed in 1993. But it is now a well-established showpiece and has been named by the Ministry of Education and Cultural Affairs as a *Patrimoine du XXe siècle*. The apartments, ranging in size from 270 to 1185 square feet, can fetch up to a million euros depending on their location. Many, however, can be rented on a weekly basis.

Address 06270 Villeneuve-Loubet | **Getting there** Villeneuve-Loubet lies about six miles southwest of Nice on the coastal road (M 6098). | **Tip** On the French Riviera, the architect André Minangoy also designed the Vista Palace Hotel overlooking Monaco (www.vistapalace.com).

111_Musée Escoffier

A museum dedicated to the founder of haute cuisine

Villeneuve-Loubet is a quiet hamlet located between Antibes and Nice. Located slightly away from the sea, it boasts within its borders a crenellated castle, a church, and a nice market square. Otherwise there is only the average, everyday ambiance of a small country town. Nightlife? Not a chance.

It was even quieter 150 years ago, here along the banks of the Loup River, than it is today. One can imagine it was downright boring for little Auguste Escoffier. And so, from a very early age, the boy stood at the stove alongside his grandmother and helped her with the cooking. When he was 13, he began an apprenticeship in his uncle's restaurant, and started his steady rise to fame: just five years later, Escoffier debuted as the Chef de Cuisine at the Hôtel Bellevue in Nice. Over the subsequent decades, he cooked in the most famous hotels in the world, including the Ritz in Paris and London's Carlton Hotel. He also ran hotel kitchens in New York City and Pittsburgh, and served as executive chef for the Hamburg America Line.

Escoffier, who was born in Villeneuve-Loubet on October 28, 1846, affected the reputation of French cuisine like no other chef; he is regarded as the originator of *haute cuisine*. At the same time, Escoffier sought to simplify and harmonize the nuances of flavor: his peach Melba, for instance – named after the opera singer Nellie Melba – balanced out the taste of a fresh peach with vanilla ice cream by adding pureed raspberries.

A few decades ago, the village of Villeneuve-Loubet opened a museum dedicated to *haute cuisine* in the house where Auguste Escoffier was born. Countless menus, cookbooks, and pieces of culinary equipment are displayed in its various rooms. An authentically equipped Provençal kitchen from the 19th century is not to be missed.

Address 3 Rue Escoffier, 06270 Villeneuve-Loubet, www.fondation-escoffier.org | **Getting there** Villeneuve-Loubet lies about six miles southwest of Nice on the coastal road (M 6098). | **Hours** Sep, Oct, Dec–June, daily 2–6pm; July and Aug, daily 2–7pm, and Mon, Tue, Thu, Fri, Sun also 10am–12pm, closed in Nov | **Tip** Auguste Escoffier died in 1935 in Monte Carlo. He was buried in the monumental family vault in the village cemetery of Villeneuve-Loubet.

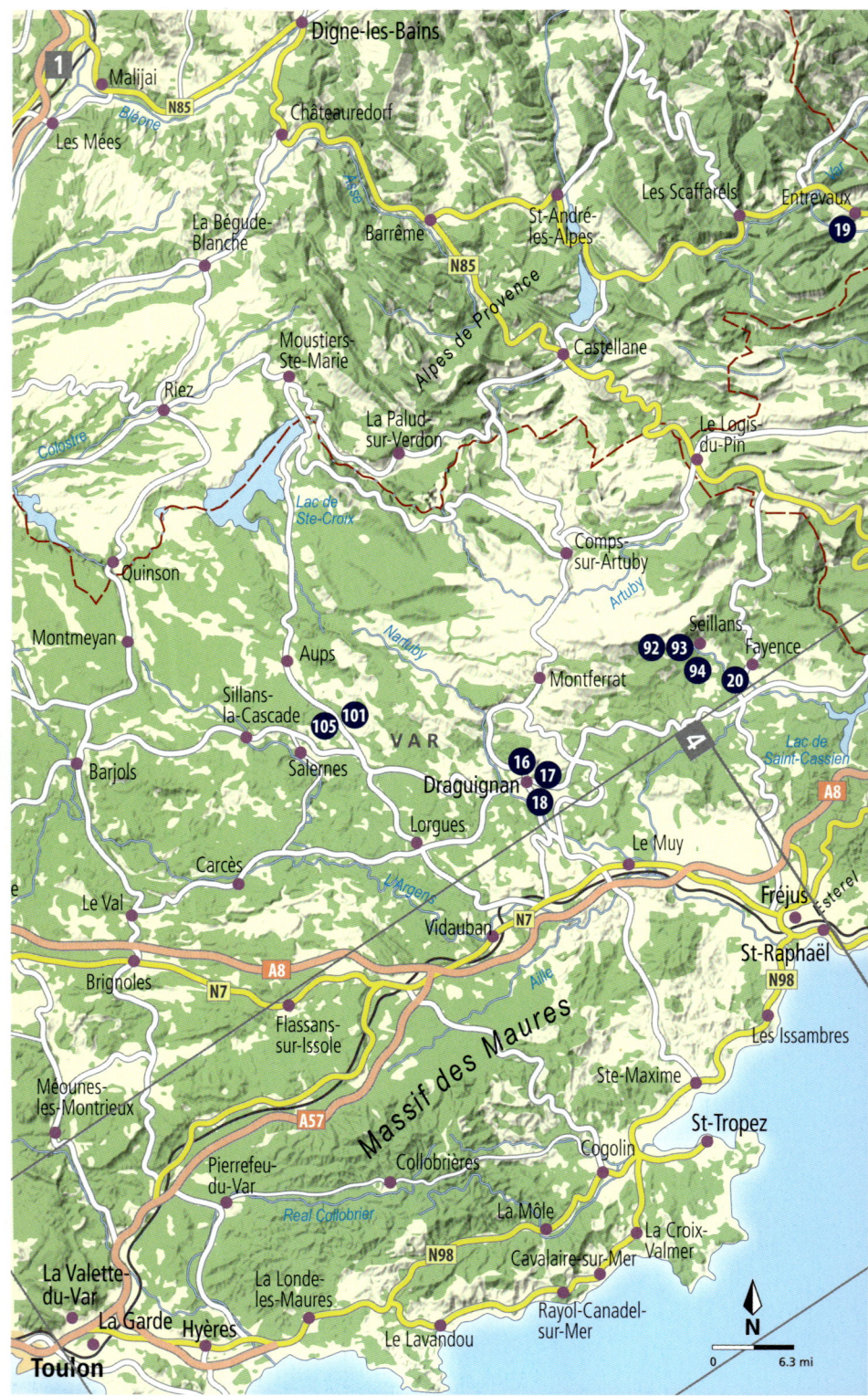

Guillaumes

St.-Sauveur-sur-Tinée

36

St.-Martin-Vésubie

79

97 96

2

75

La Brigue

33

24

Daluis

32

40

Saorge

91

La Bollène-Vésubie

95

Moulinet

4

Breil-sur-Roya

5

Puget-Théniers

Touët-sur-Var

Villars-sur-Var

68

N202

99

ITALY

Utelle

102

ALPES MARITIMES

3

Sospel

Gréolières

N202

Carros

Ventimiglia

A8

Monaco

N85

Nice

Grasse

A8

Cannes

N7

Agay

N

0   6.3 mi

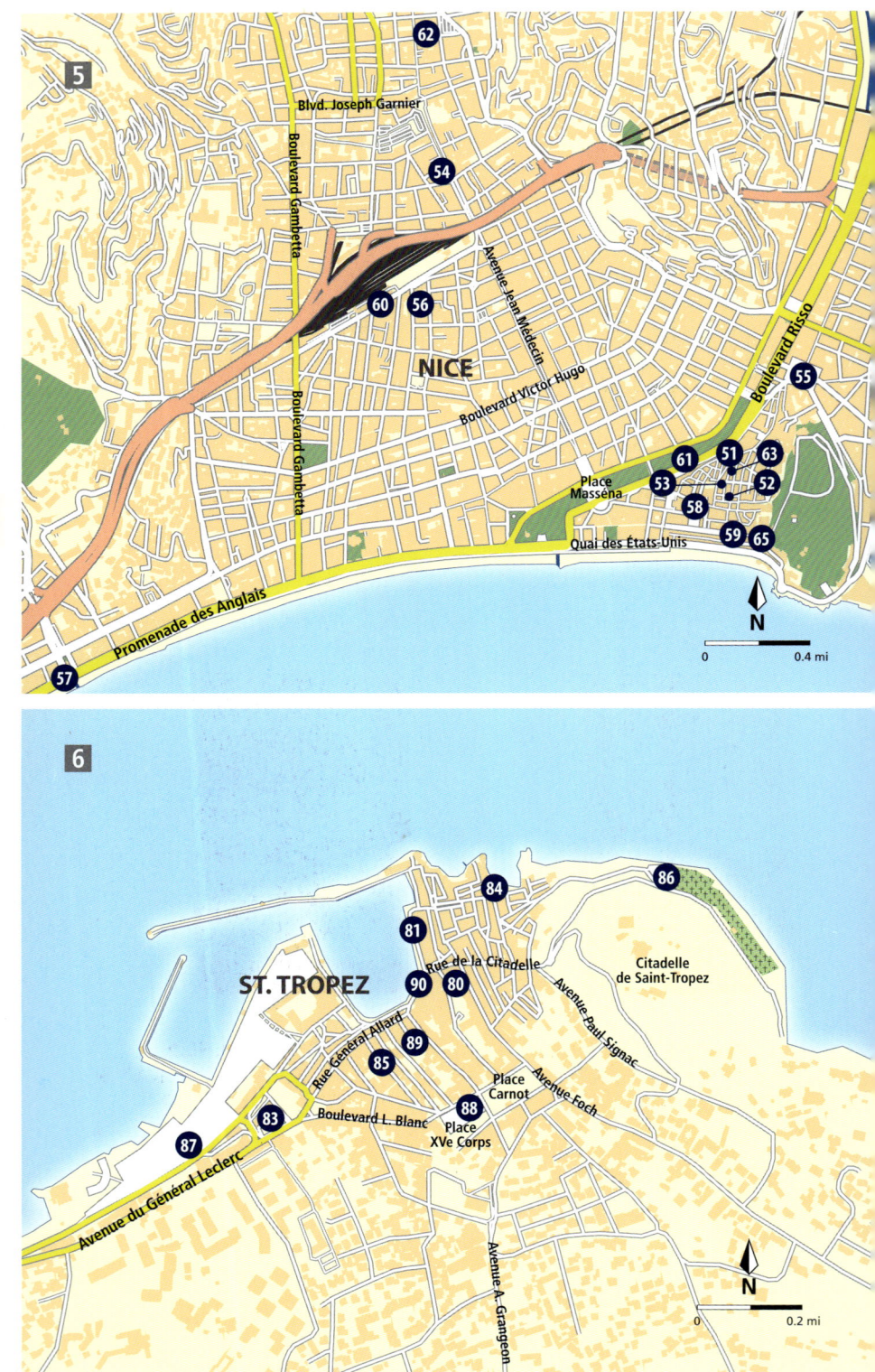

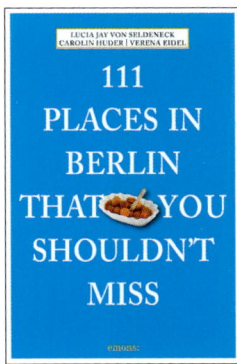

Lucia Jay von Seldeneck,
Carolin Huder, Verena Eidel
**111 PLACES IN BERLIN
THAT YOU SHOULDN'T MISS**
ISBN 978-3-95451-208-9

Rüdiger Liedtke
**111 PLACES IN MUNICH
THAT YOU SHOULDN'T MISS**
ISBN 978-3-95451-222-5

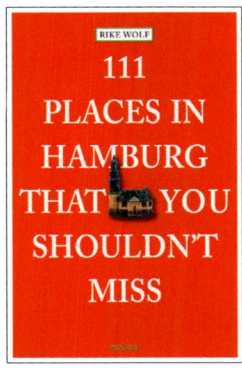

Rike Wolf
**111 PLACES IN HAMBURG
THAT YOU SHOULDN'T MISS**
ISBN 978-3-95451-234-8

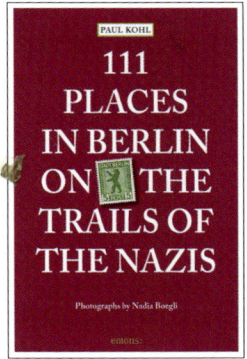

Paul Kohl
**111 PLACES IN BERLIN
ON THE TRAIL OF THE NAZIS**
ISBN 978-3-95451-323-9

Rüdiger Liedtke
**111 PLACES ON MALLORCA
THAT YOU SHOULDN'T MISS**
ISBN 978-3-95451-281-2

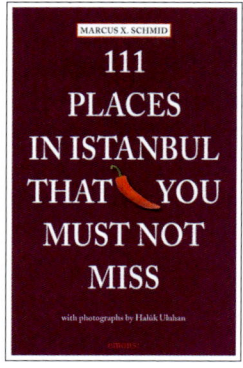

Marcus X. Schmid
**111 PLACES IN ISTANBUL
THAT YOU MUST NOT MISS**
ISBN 978-3-95451-423-6

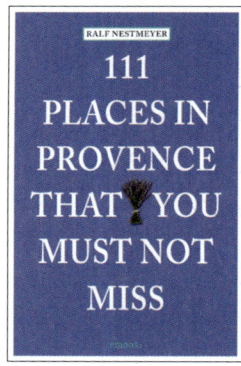

Ralf Nestmeyer
**111 PLACES IN PROVENCE
THAT YOU MUST NOT MISS**
ISBN 978-3-95451-422-9

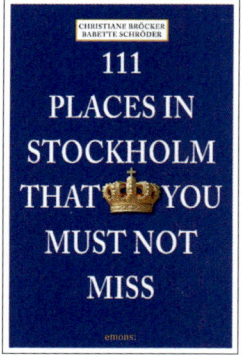

Christiane Bröcker,
Babette Schröder
**111 PLACES IN STOCKHOLM
THAT YOU MUST NOT MISS**
ISBN 978-3-95451-459-5

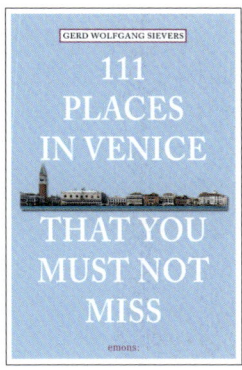

Gerd Wolfgang Sievers
**111 PLACES IN VENICE
THAT YOU MUST NOT MISS**
ISBN 978-3-95451-460-1

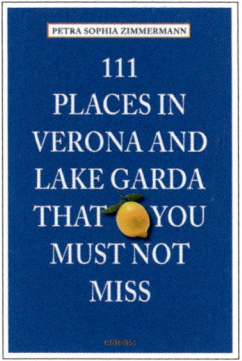

Petra Sophia Zimmermann
**111 PLACES IN VERONA
AND LAKE GARDA THAT
YOU MUST NOT MISS**
ISBN 978-3-95451-611-7

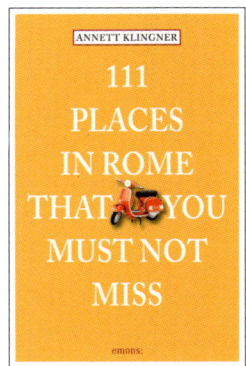

Annett Klingner
**111 PLACES IN ROME
THAT YOU MUST NOT MISS**
ISBN 978-3-95451-469-4

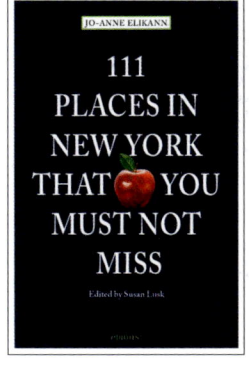

Jo-Anne Elikann
**111 PLACES IN NEW YORK
THAT YOU MUST NOT MISS**
ISBN 978-3-95451-052-8

Acknowledgments

My thanks go out to Atout France, the Comité Régional du Tourisme Provence-Alpes-Côte d'Azur, and the tourism organizations of the Départements for their help and support, in particular Susanne Zurn-Seiler, Ralph Schetter, and Monika Fritsch. A further special thank-you to Monika Ettl.

About the Author

Ralf Nestmeyer is a historian, writer, and author of several guidebooks about the South of France and Provence, including *111 Places in Provence That You Must Not Miss* (Emons Verlag). Furthermore, he has authored a book entitled *French Poets and their Houses* (Insel Verlag), as well as a literary travel guide to Provence and the Côte d'Azur (Klett-Cotta Verlag). His Provence-based crime novel *Roter Lavendel* (Red Lavender), was published by Emons Verlag. www.nestmeyer.de.